高等院校法律英语专业统编教材
"一带一路"建设涉外法律人才培养核心教材

基 础
法律英语教程

BASIC LEGAL ENGLISH

张法连 主编

北京大学出版社
PEKING UNIVERSITY PRESS

图书在版编目(CIP)数据

基础法律英语教程 / 张法连主编 . —北京：北京大学出版社，2017.5
ISBN 978-7-301-28206-9

Ⅰ.①基… Ⅱ.①张… Ⅲ.①法律 – 英语 – 高等职业教育 – 教材 Ⅳ.D9

中国版本图书馆 CIP 数据核字 (2017) 第 063239 号

书　　名	基础法律英语教程
	JICHU FALÜ YINGYU JIAOCHENG
著作责任者	张法连　主编
责任编辑	刘文静
标准书号	ISBN 978-7-301-28206-9
出版发行	北京大学出版社
地　　址	北京市海淀区成府路 205 号　100871
网　　址	http://www.pup.cn　新浪微博：@北京大学出版社
电子邮箱	编辑部 pupwaiwen@pup.cn　总编室 zpup@pup.cn
电　　话	邮购部 62752015　发行部 62750672　编辑部 62754382
印 刷 者	北京市科星印刷有限责任公司
经 销 者	新华书店
	787 毫米 ×1092 毫米　16 开本　13.75 印张　200 千字
	2017 年 5 月第 1 版　2023 年 11 月第 5 次印刷
定　　价	48.00 元

未经许可，不得以任何方式复制或抄袭本书之部分或全部内容。
版权所有，侵权必究
举报电话：010-62752024　电子邮箱：fd@pup.cn
图书如有印装质量问题，请与出版部联系，电话：010-62756370

编委会

主　编
　　张法连　（中国政法大学）

编　委
　　奚　洁　（南京大学）
　　朱　洁　（河南财经政法大学）
　　方　萍　（浙江工业大学）
　　侯雪丽　（山东管理学院）

前　言

随着中国经济和社会的迅速发展,涉外法律工作的重要性日益突显。十八届四中全会提出加强涉外法律工作;司法部、商务部、外交部和国务院法制办联合印发了《关于发展涉外法律服务业的意见》,对大力发展涉外法律服务业做出全面部署。中国已正式进入了法律服务的全球化时代。"一带一路"倡仪成为国际合作的新平台,其实质是国家的重大涉外经济工程。涉外法律工作是涉外经济活动的重要保障,法律英语则是完成涉外法律工作不可或缺的工具。"一带一路"建设离不开法律英语的保驾护航。同时,随着高校外语教学改革不断深化,法律英语已成为ESP最重要的分支之一,许多高校在外语院系开设了法律英语课程或设置了法律英语方向,收到了良好的社会效果。培养能够适应法律服务国际化要求的复合型涉外法律人才是时代发展的必然需要。

法律英语是法律科学与英语语言学有机结合产生的一门实践性很强的交叉学科。在专门用途英语(English for Specific Purposes)中,法律英语最具特色。法律用语和法律文件等都具有鲜明的特点,要求采用严格的、规范的、正式的语体。法律文化的差异也对法律语言的理解造成了障碍,这些都对英语语言的掌握和运用提出了更高的要求。法律英语的教学就是为了满足这一专门需要而应运而生的。法律英语对于法律人外有人的重要性不言而喻,掌握法律英语,就等于突破了国内相对狭窄的地域限制,展翅高翔,可以让我们"飞得更高,看得更远",从而从容接轨全球法律服务市场。

本教材主要是以介绍美国法为主线。美国法是英美法系的典型代表,其法律体系完整、内容丰富,既有传统的普通法,又有新兴的成文法;既有统一的联邦法,又有各州的法律。同时,美国法在世界范围内影响深远,很多国家都在研究、借鉴其做法,许多国际公约也参照美国法的理念、原则和规则制订。通过本教材的学习,既能学习以美国法为代表的西方法律知识,又可以提高在涉外法律这一特定领域内的英语听、说、读、写、译的技能。

此外,本教材还具有以下特点:

首先,针对法律英语初学者,本教材的内容较之其他法律英语教材更为简单和浓缩,容易接受。教材前四章以对话这一日常的语言形式来导入,初步展示了法律英语运用的语言环境和语体特征，简单介绍了普通法常见的法律关系和法律概念。随后以篇章的形式由浅入深地介绍了法律文化和美国的部门法。在阅读材料的选取中，本教材特别注意选取难度适中的材料，确保绝大多数初学者可以轻松阅读。

其次，本教材对英美法律文化进行了系统介绍，包括法庭礼仪和服饰、遵循先例、律师的职业和道德、普通法和成文法传统、陪审团制度、法院系统、法律教育等等。语言是文化的载体，法律英语的学习不能忽视英美法律文化知识。

再次，本教材设计编写体系完备。在介绍了英美法律文化之后，又用十个章节的篇幅介绍了美国主要的部门法，如宪法、合同法、侵权法、物权法、证据法、知识产权法、刑法、刑事程序法、民事程序法和商法。考虑到"一带一路"建设的实际需要，本教材还增加了对WTO制度的简单介绍。

本教材在每章节后都附有相关的练习题，以帮助学习者检查课堂内容的掌握程度，查漏补缺。在编写本书的过程中，我们参考了大量国内外有关资料，在此谨对原作者表示诚挚的感谢。

Contents

UNIT 1   REPORTING A CRIME   1
UNIT 2   CONSULTING A LAWYER   4
UNIT 3   ARBITRATION   7
UNIT 4   PLEA BARGAINING   11
UNIT 5   CHARACTERISTICS OF LEGAL ENGLISH   14
UNIT 6   DOCTRINE OF STARE DECISIS   19
UNIT 7   COURT ETIQUETTE AND ATTIRE   23
UNIT 8   LEGAL ETHICS   27
UNIT 9   CHIEF JUSTICE IN THE UNITED STATES   31
UNIT 10   LAWYERS   35
UNIT 11   COMMON LAW & CIVIL LAW SYSTEM   40
UNIT 12   JURY TRIAL   47
UNIT 13   COURT SYSTEM IN THE UNITED STATES   53
UNIT 14   SOURCES OF LAW IN THE UNITED STATES   58
UNIT 15   SEVEN PRINCIPLES IN THE U.S. JUDICIAL SYSTEM   63
UNIT 16   LEGAL PROFESSIONALS IN THE UNITED STATES   68
UNIT 17   LEGAL AID IN THE UNITED STATES   74
UNIT 18   LEGAL EDUCATION IN THE UNITED STATES   81
UNIT 19   WORLD TRADE ORGANIZATION (I)   88

UNIT 20	WORLD TRADE ORGANIZATION (II)	96
UNIT 21	CONSTITUTIONAL LAW	103
UNIT 22	CONTRACTS	109
UNIT 23	TORTS	116
UNIT 24	PROPERTY LAW	123
UNIT 25	EVIDENCE LAW	130
UNIT 26	INTELLECTUAL PROPERTY LAW	136
UNIT 27	CRIMINAL LAW	142
UNIT 28	CRIMINAL PROCEDURE	150
UNIT 29	CIVIL PROCEDURE	157
UNIT 30	BUSINESS LAW	164

KEY TO THE EXERCISES 170

APPENDIX A HOW TO BRIEF CASES AND ANALYZE CASE PROBLEMS 187

APPENDIX B HOW TO READ A U.S. SUPREME COURT OPINION 194

APPENDIX C TRANSCRIPT OF A RECORDING OF A TELEPHONE CONVERSATION BETWEEN THE PRESIDENT AND H.R. HALDEMAN, THE WHITE HOUSE TELEPHONE, APRIL 19, 1973, FROM 9:37 P.M. TO 9:53 P.M. 199

UNIT 1
REPORTING A CRIME

(A woman goes into a police office to report a crime.)

A= Police officer; B=Woman

A: Can I help you?

B: I want to report a crime, sir.

A: What's happened?

B: I can't find my car. Somebody must have stolen it about 40 minutes ago.

A: Where did you park the car?

B: On the parking lot at the entrance to the post office.

A: Where's the post office? The specific address, I mean.

B: It's on Zhongshan Road, just the **opposite** to the Bank of China. There's a **crossroads** nearby. But I don't quite remember the street number.

A: Where did you go after parking the car?

B: I went to the post office to mail a **package**. It was probably ten twenty at that time. There were many people **queuing** in the office. So it took me nearly 30 minutes to finish the work. When I went out of the gate, I found my car disappeared.

A: Could you please describe the car? What type of car is it?

B: It's a Toyota 2000. I bought it in 1998.

A: What's the color?

B: Light brown.

A: And the number of the **license plate**?

B: AX11211.

A: OK. We'll start the **investigation** at once. We'll contact you as soon as it's found.

Please leave your name and your phone number.

B: Thank you, sir.

New Words & Expressions

opposite	[ˈɒpəzɪt]	*adj.*	相反的；对面的；对立的
		n.	对立面
crossroad	[ˈkrɒsˌrəʊd]	*n.*	十字路口；交叉路；岔道
package	[ˈpækɪdʒ]	*n.*	包裹
queue	[kjuː]	*vi.*	排队；排队等候
		n.	队列；长队
license plate	[ˈlaɪsəns pleɪt]	*n.*	牌照
investigation	[ɪnˌvestɪˈgeɪʃn]	*n.*	调查

Exercises

I. Translate the following dialogue.

A: 警察先生，我要报案。

B: 发生了什么事?

A: 我的手提包被抢了?

B: 什么时候被抢的?

A: 就在刚才，大概15分钟以前。

B: 在哪里被抢的? 怎么被抢的?

A: 我去超市买东西，刚走出门口没几步，有个男的从我身后一把抢过我的手提包就跑。我想追上去，可他一会儿就不见了。

B: 你的手提包是什么样的?

A: 是个粉红色的手提包，幸运鸭牌的，还很新。挎带上还系一个钥匙扣。

B: 手提包里装有什么东西?

A: 装有钱包、手提电话、一把黑色的雨伞。钱包里有 300 元,还有工作证和身份证。

B: 那个男的长得什么样? 你能描述一下吗?

A: 不太高,瘦瘦的,留有胡子。

B: 穿什么样的衣服? 什么颜色的?

A: 白色的长袖上衣,深蓝色的牛仔裤。我不太肯定。

B: 就这些,还有什么要补充吗?

A: 没有了。我就记得这么多。

B: 好的。把你的姓名、住址和联系方式留下来。我们会尽快展开调查,一有消息就通知你。

II. Role-play

Work in pairs, making up dialogues according to the following situation: You are walking home in the evening. The street is quiet. A man behind you takes out a knife, threatening you to surrender all your possessions to him. You have no choice but to obey. After he runs away, you go to the police station to report the hold-up. Take turns to be the victim and the police officer.

UNIT 2
CONSULTING A LAWYER

(A person form a joint- venture company goes to a law office to hire a lawyer who can represent his company in a lawsuit.)

A= lawyer; B=client

A: Is there anything I can do for you, sir?

B: Yes. Our company is engaged in a lawsuit concerning international trade. We'd like to engage a lawyer to act on our behalf. Could you tell me if we can engage a lawyer from your law firm?

A: I think you've come to the right place. To be honest, we have rich experience in handling cases involving foreign-related matters. We have a lot of excellent lawyers who have both a good command of English and legal expertise.

B: Really? That's wonderful. What if we'd like to engage your firm to act on our behalf?

A: Our practice is we will have a face-to-face talk about the case and lawyer fee first. After we reach a **consensus**, you'll be presented with a formatted agreement of **entrusted** agency for your reading and signature.

B: What's the agreement about?

A: It includes without limitation entrusted matters, lawyer's mode of work, **sphere** and description of **authorization** by the client, sum and mode of payment, **default**, terms of **revocation** and settlement of disputes, etc.

B: Can I have a look at a sample agreement?

A: Sure. Here it is.

B: If there's disagreement as to the terms **stipulated** in the agreement, is there any possibility of making changes?

UNIT 2
CONSULTING A LAWYER

A: Yes. As I said earlier, the agreement is based on what we agree on.

B: I see. After concluding the agreement, what shall I do?

A: You must present us with a power of **attorney**.

B: What do you mean by a power of attorney?

A: A power of attorney is a legal instrument which specifies matters, terms and scope of attorney.

B: Anything else?

A: Then perform your obligation of paying the bill and cooperating with your lawyer and meantime enjoy your lawful rights in your **litigation** or non-litigation process.

B: I see.

A: OK. Please feel free to contact me if you have any question.

B: Thank you for your information and time.

New Words & Expressions

consensus	[kənˈsensəs]	n.	一致；舆论；一致同意,合
entrust	[ɪnˈtrʌst]	vt.	委托,托付
sphere	[sfɪə(r)]	n.	球(体)；(兴趣或活动的)范围；势力范围；天体,如行星或恒星
		vt.	形成球体；包围,围绕；置于球面内部
authorization	[ˌɔːθəraɪˈzeɪʃn]	n.	授权,批准；批准(或授权)的证
default	[dɪˈfɔːlt]	vi.	未履行任务或责任；受传唤时未出庭；由于不到庭而败诉；弃权
		vt.	未履行,拖欠；未参加或完成(例如,比赛)；[法]因未到庭而败(诉)
		n.	未履行,拖欠；[法]未到庭；弃权；[计]缺省,默认

revocation	[ˌrevəˈkeɪʃn]	n.	废止,撤回
stipulate	[ˈstɪpjuleɪt]	vt.	(尤指在协议或建议中)规定,约定,讲明(条件等)
		vi.	规定,明确要求
attorney	[əˈtɜːnɪ]	n.	代理人;律师
litigation	[ˌlɪtɪˈgeɪʃn]	n.	(律)打官司;诉讼

Exercises

I. Change the sentences to a more polite form.

1. Be sure to arrive on time for your scheduled appointment.
2. Is there any possibility of winning the case?
3. What do I do if I just cannot afford a quality lawyer?
4. Please recommend a good lawyer to me.
5. Tell me when the court will hear this case.

II. Role-play

Work in pairs; try to give your advice or recommendation for the following situations: Your cooperating partner fails to perform its contractual obligations.

UNIT 3
ARBITRATION

(A client is considering an alternative resolution to the traditional court process in his dispute. He is consulting his attorney about the settlement.)

A= Attorney; B=client

A: What's your problem?

B: I decide not to go to court. You know it often takes lots of time and money to go to court. May I have any other options?

A: Of course, you may turn to **ADR**.

B: Excuse me, what do you mean by ADR?

A: It stands for Alternative Dispute Resolution to the traditional court process.

B: That's exactly what I'm interested in. Is it a new thing?

A: No. Alternative Dispute Resolution is not a new idea in the judicial system. Most parties settle civil cases before going to court. Courts often use a variety of techniques to bring about voluntary cases before going to court. Courts often use a variety of techniques to bring about voluntary settlement such as pre-trial settlement conferences, **mediation** by **magistrates**, court-related **arbitration**, and mediation in the judge's **chambers**, etc.

B: Then which forms do people most often use?

A: It really depends on the individuals. Generally the local dispute resolution centers offer two forms of negotiation: mediation and arbitration.

B: What does each of these methods involve?

A: Mediation is used primarily in labor-management grievances. It helps the parties reach an agreement and offers recommendations for settlement. The recommendations are not binding on the parties. The function of mediation is basically advisory.

B: How about arbitration?

A: Arbitration should be distinguished from mediation. Arbitration is an important method of resolving commercial disputes out of court. The award of the arbitrator is final and binding on the parties. Arbitration performs a judicial function and decides disputes between parties.

B: What types of cases use arbitration most often?

A: Commercial, insurance, and labor-management disagreements widely use arbitration.

B: So is arbitration applied to my case?

A: Yes of course. Your case concerns a commercial contract. Arbitration is applicable.

B: Compared with court proceedings, is arbitration a better method to resolve a dispute?

A: It's hard to say which is better. Both have advantages and disadvantages. Arbitration may be less formal, but less complex, and less costly than court cases. And it has privacy, and often ends more quickly. Although it does not replace the court, arbitration is an effective **alternative** to formal court **litigation** in certain types of **controversies**.

B: How about mediation then?

A: Mediation is an informal process where a mediator helps those involved resolve their problems by identifying, defining, and discussing the things about which they disagree. It has privacy and speedy resolution. But it is not binding or enforceable.

B: Well, I prefer to use arbitration to settle my dispute.

New Words & Expressions

ADR: "Alternative Dispute Resolution"的缩写, 替代性纠纷解决方式; 替代性争议解决机制; 替代性纠纷解决机制; 非诉讼纠纷解决机制; 替代性纠纷解决。

mediation [ˌmiːdɪˈeɪʃn] n. 调停, 调解, 斡旋

magistrate [ˈmædʒɪstreɪt] n. 地方法官, 治安官; 文职官员; 治安推事

arbitration	[ˌɑːbɪˈtreɪʃn]	n.	仲裁，公断
chamber	[ˈtʃeɪmbə(r)]	n.	室，卧室，会客室；内庭；（多用于英国）律师的办公室；议事厅
		vt.	限制，幽禁，封闭或限制；使备有房间
alternative	[ɔːlˈtɜːnətɪv]	adj.	替代的；备选的；其他的；另类的
		n.	可供选择的事物
litigation	[ˌlɪtɪˈɡeɪʃn]	n.	（律）打官司；诉讼
controversy	[ˈkɒntrəvɜːsi]	n.	公开辩论；论战

Exercises

I. Interpret the following dialogue.

A: I had some disputes in business with Peter. I was wondering how to settle them? What's your opinion, Mr. White?

B: Do you want to sue him?

A: If I go to court, it will take me lots of time and energy. Time is money, you know. What's more, Peter is my old client. I don't want to break our relationship. Any other options?

B: Yes. Have you ever heard about ADR before?

A: Yes. It seems to refer to Alternative Dispute Resolution to the traditional court process.

B: Yes. It has many forms including arbitration, mediation, and negotiation and so on. You can think them over.

A: Which one is better?

B: Each has both advantage and disadvantage. It depends on the situation. Generally, mediation is used primarily in labor-management grievances. It helps the parties reach an agreement and offer recommendations for settlement, but the recommendations are not binding on the parties.

II. Role-play

Work in small groups, trying to make a debate. Each group consists of seven students. One student acts as the chairman. The other six students are divided into two parties, party A and party B. Party A's position is that arbitration is a better method to settle a dispute. Party B's position is that mediation is a better method to settle a dispute. Finally the best group and the best debater are to be selected.

UNIT 4
PLEA BARGAINING

*(An agreement on **plea bargaining** has been reached between the district attorney and defense counsel. They submit the agreement to the judge for approval. After the consent of the judge the case is settled without **indictment** and jury trial.)*

(APPRARANCE: District Attorney,

        Appearing on behalf of the People.

        Defense Counsel,

        Appearing on behalf of the Defendant.

        Before

        Judge John Gates)

(DA=District Attorney   D=Defendant   DC=Defense Counsel   J=Judge)

DA: Your Honor, the defendant, who is here in court, prepared to waive indictment and plead guilty to Superior Court Information charging **sodomy** in the 3rd degree. He's doing this with the understanding that I have discussed this with his defense counsel, who has presented to me certain medical information that would lead me to believe it would not be prudent to have the defendant serve a jail term. I'm recommending that, as part of our plea bargain, upon his plea he will not serve a jail term. The balance of the sentence is up to the Court.

J: I see, but if that's recommended by the Probation Department, there may be the condition of electronic monitoring.

DC: That's fine, Your Honor. I would note that my client has some serious medical conditions now, which would preclude him from going to trial, and that's a good part of the reason why we're accepting the plea offer today.

J: Okay. I do approve the **waiver** of indictment. Mr. Defendant, the District Attorney has filed a Superior Court Information, charging you with sodomy in the 3rd degree. Do you understand what the attorneys have said just now?

D: Yes.

J: You know that you have a right to a jury trial on this charge?

D: I do.

J: By pleading guilty, you're giving up that right. Do you realize that?

D: I do.

J: That means you're giving up the right to have the witnesses against you produced in the Court, to have your lawyer **cross-examine** those witnesses and to present any defense you may have. Do you understand this?

D: Yes.

J: How do you **plead**?

D: Guilty.

New Words & Expressions

plea bargaining	[pliːˈbɑːgənɪŋ]	n.	控辩交易
indictment	[ɪnˈdaɪtmənt]	n.	诉状,起诉书；〈尤美〉刑事起诉书；控告, 起诉
sodomy	[ˈsɒdəmɪ]	n.	鸡奸
waiver	[ˈweɪvə(r)]	n.	弃权；放弃；弃权声明书
cross-examine	[ˌkrɔːsɪgˈzæmɪn, ˌkrɒs-]		
		vt.	对……盘问,仔细的盘问；〈律〉向(对方证人)反讯问
		vi.	仔细盘问某人

UNIT 4
PLEA BARGAINING

plead	[pli:d]	vi.	恳求；辩论
		vt.	以……为理由；陈述案情；申辩，认罪，辩护
		vt.& vi.	申诉，答辩，为……辩护
guilty	['gɪlti]	adj.	内疚的；有罪的

Exercises

I. Choose the proper words from the list below to fill in the blanks. Change the form of the words if necessary.

> lenient / serious / criminal / guilty / conviction
> lengthy / concession / original / dismissal / prosecutor

A plea bargain is any agreement in a ___1___ case between the ___2___ and defendant whereby the defendant agrees to plead guilty to a particular charge in return for some ___3___ from the prosecutor. This may mean that the defendant will plead ___4___ to a less serious charge, or to one of several charges, in return for the ___5___ of other charges; or it may mean that the defendant will plead guilty to the ___6___ criminal charge in return for a more ___7___ sentence. A plea bargain allows both parties to avoid a ___8___ criminal trial and may allow criminal defendants to avoid the risk of ___9___ at trial on a more ___10___ charge.

II. Comprehensive Questions

1. Why are defendants willing to plead guilty instead of a jury trial in criminal cases?
2. In what way are most felony cases resolved?
3. What are the three categories of explicit plea bargaining?
4. Why do prosecutors over-charge the accused at the stage of plea bargaining?
5. How can the knowledge at a case was not settled by a bargain influence the sentencing decisions of the judge?

UNIT 5
CHARACTERISTICS OF LEGAL ENGLISH

Modern legal English has it root in the history of the development of English as a legal language. In prehistoric Britain, traditional common law was discussed in the **vernacular**. After the Norman Conquest of English in 1066, the common law began to develop, which, however, lacked **uniformity** and **stability**. Along with the development of written reports of the cases, the courts began to look to previously decided cases to assist them in coming to a decision and thus developed **the doctrine of stare decisis**. This doctrine of stare decisis is a major factor which has caused English to play such a pivotal role in the common law and to develop into a new sublanguage — legal English.

Legal English differs from standard international English in that it refers to the style of English used by legal professionals in their work. For example, the language used in international contracts and **statutes** can also be referred to as "**legalese**". Legal English has long been considered a necessary skill for lawyers in English-speaking countries; however, due to the **emergence** of English as the language of international business it is becoming a necessary skill for all legal international professionals to consider acquiring.

Traditionally the law has always had its own "language" used and understood only by legal professionals internationally, whether this be Latin, English, French or a combination of other languages. This legal language has changed and adapted with the various conquering countries in the past. Each influence has contributed significantly to the international language we call Legal English today and forms the basis of its distinctive style. When explored further, it is clearly possible to see how common terms in international Legal English today such as "**Will** and **Testament**" have developed from a combination of the languages that exist only in the Legal world.

UNIT 5
CHARACTERISTICS OF LEGAL ENGLISH

There are a number of differences between Legal English and standard international English. Firstly, some words in standard international English have entirely different meanings when used in a legal context. One example of this is the use of the word "**consideration**" which means thinking about others in standard international English, but when used with regard to a contract refers to the thing of value that passes between people in exchange for something. Secondly, there are the words that are only used in an international legal context and would not be used or understood in everyday life by persons without legal training such as "**tort**" and "**restrictive covenant**". There is also the distinct lack of **punctuation** in legal documents and differing word order. This would cause great confusion to a person who has only taken a standard international English course and had no understanding of Legal English. In fact there are a number of grammatical differences, another example being the use of the word "**said**" in the phrase "the said Martin O'Leary." Finally and most obviously there is the use of words and phrases in other languages altogether, for example "stare decisis."

The **formality** of Legal English helps emphasize the importance and significance of certain international documents, for example, **declarations**. It makes the person signing the document, particularly if they are not legally trained, consider the document more carefully and appreciate the significance of it. However it must not be forgotten who the document is actually intended for; whilst the use of international Legal English will result in a formal, impressive and **intimidating** document, if it causes confusion for the **client** then neither the document nor the legal professional are correctly fulfilling their role. Someone who does not understand international Legal English will struggle to create, or interpret, a legal document that balances a need for formality with the client's requirements and understanding.

There is some international debate as to the necessity of Legal English as there is the argument that the law should be conducted in an international language that is easily understood by the general public. However as mentioned above there is the advantage that the use of Legal English gives a document an **authority** that standard international

English will not be able to do. Also, without an understanding of Legal English it would be impossible to correctly understand and interpret the extensive laws made previously.

Despite the continuing international debate regarding the use of international Legal English it is clear that it is the professional language of the legal profession and thus an important skill for any legal professional to acquire. International Legal English is **ingrained** in the profession whether this be a positive or negative thing and remaining ignorant of it will only result in a less effective and efficient legal professional.

New Words & Expressions

vernacular	[vəˈnækjələ(r)]	n.	方言，土话
uniformity	[ˌjuːnɪˈfɔːməti]	n.	一致性
stability	[stəˈbɪləti]	n.	稳定性
the doctrine of stare decisis			遵循先例的原则
statute	[ˈstætʃuːt]	n.	法规；法令；条例
legalese	[ˌliːɡəˈliːz, -ˈliːs]	n.	法律行话
emergence	[ɪˈmɜːdʒəns]	n.	出现；形成
will	[wɪl]	n.	遗嘱
testament	[ˈtestəmənt]	n.	遗嘱；证明
consideration	[kənˌsɪdəˈreɪʃn]	n.	对价；约因
tort	[tɔːt]	n.	侵权行为
restrictive covenant	[rɪˈstrɪktɪv ˈkʌvənənt]	n.	限制性条款；约束性规定
punctuation	[ˌpʌŋktʃuˈeɪʃn]	n.	标点符号
said	[sed]	adj.	（合同，申诉等）前述的
formality	[fɔːˈmæləti]	n.	正式
declaration	[ˌdekləˈreɪʃn]	n.	声明
intimidating	[ɪnˈtɪmɪdeɪtɪŋ]	adj.	令人生畏的，有震慑力的
client	[ˈklaɪənt]	n.	委托人，当事人

authority	[ɔːˈθɒrəti]	n.	权威性
ingrained	[ɪnˈɡreɪnd]	adj.	根深蒂固的

Exercises

I. Judge whether the statements below are true (T) or false (F).

1. Legal English refers to the language only used by lawyers. (   )
2. Generally speaking there is no significant difference in word meaning when some words are used in legal context and in everyday life. (   )
3. Some words in legal context can only be understood or used by legal professionals. (   )
4. In legal documents, punctuation is very important and has to be carefully used. (   )
5. Word order in legal documents should be exactly the same as what is said in grammar books that ordinary people use. (   )
6. In Legal English, there are quite a few words from other languages. (   )
7. The use of legal English in legal context is merely to intimidate clients. (   )
8. Written in legal English, the legal documents are more authoritative than ordinary writings using everyday English. (   )
9. Even if people do not have any legal training, they can understanding Legal English well because it is merely a branch of English. (   )
10. Legal English is not necessary for all legal professionals as long as they have a sound understanding of laws.

II. Use your dictionary and find out the meaning of the following words and expressions in legal context. Discuss with your classmates the meaning differences between legal context and everyday English.

1. accord
2. acquire

3. composition

4. discharge

5. enter into

6. grace

7. infant

8. principal

9. secure

10. without prejudice to

UNIT 6
DOCTRINE OF STARE DECISIS

Stare decisis (Anglo-Latin pronunciation: /ˈstɛəriː dɪˈsaɪsɪs/) is a legal principle by which judges are obligated to respect the **precedent** established by prior decisions. The words originate from the phrasing of the principle in the Latin **maxim** "Stare decisis et non **quieta** movere": to stand by decisions and not disturb the undisturbed. In a legal context, this is understood to mean that courts should generally abide by precedent and not disturb settled matters. The principle of stare decisis can be divided into two components:

The first is the rule that a decision made by a superior court, or by the same court in an earlier decision, is binding precedent that the court itself and all its inferior courts are obligated to follow; the second is the principle that a court should not overturn its own precedent unless there is a strong reason to do so and should be guided by principles from lateral and inferior courts. The second principle, regarding persuasive precedent, is an advisory one that courts can and do ignore occasionally.

Stare decisis is a legal principle of case law in common law systems. In the common law tradition, courts decide the law applicable to a case by interpreting statutes and applying precedent which record how and why prior cases have been decided. Unlike most civil law systems, common law systems follow the doctrine of stare decisis, by which most courts are bound by their own previous decisions in similar cases, and all lower courts should make decisions consistent with previous decisions of higher courts. For example, in England, the High Court and the Court of Appeal are each bound by their own previous decisions, but the Supreme Court of the United Kingdom is able to deviate from its earlier decisions, although in practice it rarely does so.

Generally speaking, higher courts do not have direct oversight over day-to-day **proceedings** in lower courts, in that they cannot reach out on their own initiative at any time to reverse or overrule judgments of the lower courts. Normally, the burden rests with litigants to **appeal** rulings (including those in clear violation of established case law) to the higher courts. If a judge acts against precedent and the case is not appealed, the decision will stand.

A lower court may not rule against a binding precedent, even if the lower court feels that the precedent is unjust; the lower court may only express the hope that a higher court or the **legislature** will reform the rule in question. If the court believes that developments or trends in legal reasoning render the precedent unhelpful, and wishes to evade it and help the law evolve, the court may either hold that the precedent is inconsistent with subsequent authority, or that the precedent should be distinguished by some material difference between the facts of the cases. If that judgment goes to appeal, the appellate court will have the opportunity to review both the precedent and the case under appeal, perhaps overruling the previous case law by setting a new precedent of higher authority. This may happen several times as the case works its way through **successive** appeals.

Any court may seek to distinguish its present case from that of a binding precedent, in order to reach a different conclusion. The validity of such a distinction may or may not be accepted on appeal. An **appellate** court may also **propound** an entirely new and different analysis from that of junior courts, and may or may not be bound by its own previous decisions, or in any case may distinguish the decisions based on significant differences in the facts applicable to each case. Or, a court may view the matter before it as one of "first impression," not governed by any controlling precedent.

New Words & Expressions

precedent ['presɪdənt] *n.* 前例；先例
　　　　　　　　　　　　adj. 在前的, 在先的

UNIT 6
DOCTRINE OF STARE DECISIS

maxim	['mæksɪm]	n.	格言，座右铭；准则
proceeding	[prə'si:dɪŋ]	n.	进行，进程；行动；诉讼；会议记录
		v.	进行（proceed 的现在分词）；前进；（沿特定路线）行进；（尤指打断后）继续说
appeal	[ə'pi:l]	n.	上诉；[体育]诉请；呼吁；（迫切的）要求（帮助、同情等）恳求
legislature	['ledʒɪsleɪtʃə(r)]	n.	立法机关；立法机构；立法部；（特指）州议会
		vi.	（迫切）要求；有吸引力；求助（于）；提请注意
		vt.	将……移交上级法院审理
successive	[sək'sesɪv]	adj.	连续的，相继的；继承的，接替的；逐次
appellate	[ə'pelɪt]	adj.	（尤指法庭）上诉的，受理上诉的
propound	[prə'paʊnd]	vt.	提出（问题、计划等）供考虑（讨论），提议

Exercises

I. Choose the best answer for each of the following questions.

1. Stare decisis means _____.

   A. all necessary changes having been made

   B. to stand by that which is decided

   C. by the court (said of a decision not identifying the judge who wrote it)

   D. not with standing the verdict

2. Which of the following is NOT true?

   A. Stare decisis is a Latin term meaning "to stand by that which is decided."

   B. A lower court may not rule against a binding precedent.

   C. Stare decisis has never been overruled by courts in some cases.

   D. Stare decisis is a doctrine or policy of following rules or principles laid down in previous judicial decisions.

3. Stare decisis is a legal principle _____.

A. in America

B. in Japan

C. in China

D. in Germany

II. Choose the proper words from the list below to fill in the blanks. Change the form of the words if necessary.

> essence / identical / Latin / disregard / trial
> future / hear / decision / prior / appellate

Stare decisis is a ___1___ term meaning "to stand by that which is decided." It is a legal principle which dictates that courts cannot ___2___ the standard. The court must uphold ___3___ decisions. In ___4___, this legal principle dictates that once a law has been determined by the ___5___ court (which ___6___ and determines appeals from the ___7___ of the ___8___ courts) to be relevant to the facts of the case, ___9___ cases will follow the same principle of law if they involve considerably ___10___ facts.

UNIT 7
COURT ETIQUETTE AND ATTIRE

What you wear and how you act always matters, especially when appearing in court. If you think your attitude or appearance doesn't matter, consider that they may cause you to be cited for **contempt** of court. Whether you are the **plaintiff** or the defendant, or even a witness in a lawsuit, your appearance, dress, and actions can affect how the court sees you and how successful you are in presenting your case.

Respect for the Court is of ultimate significance. A courtroom is a **solemn** place, representing the judicial branch of the government, and a judge demands respect as a representative of the government, whether it is federal, state, or local. Specific rules apply to those who are bringing cases to court or who have cases brought against them. In fact, anyone appearing before the court, including witnesses and members of the public, has the responsibility to act with respect.

You must have respect for the judge as a representative of the court, and respect for the courtroom process. Here are some general rules that most courts require you to comply with if you are in court.

- Arrive early and prepared. You might have to sit and wait, but that is far better than running late. Arrive late and you might find your case passed by.
- Wear business clothing; no wild hairstyles, open shoes, tank tops, mini skirts, T shirts, or other non-business **attire**.
- Gum chewing, tobacco, recording devices, cell phones, food, beverages, or newspapers are NOT allowed.
- Cell phones are not allowed in many courtrooms. If you are permitted to bring your cell phone, TURN IT OFF!

- Don't wear a hat unless it is for religious reasons.
- Children are allowed in most courtrooms, but only if they are quiet. If you must bring your children, have someone with you who can take the child out if he or she becomes loud or **disruptive**.
- In general, you must have permission to move beyond a certain point toward the judge or jury. For example, if you are called as a witness, you will be sworn in. You may not move out of the witness box without permission. If you are sitting at the defense or **prosecution** table with your attorney, you may not move forward without permission.
- The judge is to be addressed as "Your Honor," not "Judge Smith." Talk only to the judge and (in a soft voice) to your attorney. Do not address the opposing counsel or other party. When referring to others, do not use first names. It's "Mr. Smith," not "Jim," even if he is your brother-in-law.
- Speak only when instructed or given permission. Don't interrupt. When you answer questions, be brief and to the point; answer the question you were asked and stop.
- Don't interrupt anyone, most especially not the judge.
- Only one person speaks at a time, because of recording devices in the courtroom and for politeness.
- Don't argue, especially not with the judge.
- Use formal English, not **slang**.

In other words, be on your best behavior and consider the solemnity of the courtroom. Show respect to the judge and others in the courtroom.

New Words & Expressions

etiquette	[ˈetɪket]	n.	礼仪，礼节；规矩；礼数
contempt	[kənˈtempt]	n.	轻视，蔑视

UNIT 7
COURT ETIQUETTE AND ATTIRE

plaintiff	[ˈpleɪntɪf]	n.	原告
solemn	[ˈsɒləm]	adj.	庄严的, 严肃的
solemnity	[səˈlemnəti]	n.	庄严, 严肃
attire	[əˈtaɪə(r)]	n.	服装, 服饰
disruptive	[dɪsˈrʌptɪv]	adj.	破坏性的
prosecution	[ˌprɒsɪˈkjuːʃn]	n.	起诉, 检举
slang	[slæŋ]	n.	俚语, 行话

Exercises

I. Judge whether the statements below are true (T) or false (F).

1. Even if our attitude or clothing are improper, we will not judged by our appearance in court. (   )

2. The appearance is particularly important for a defendant than for a witness. (   )

3. Federal court has higher requirements about clothing than state courts. (   )

4. Anyone appearing before the court including legal professionals should act with respect. (   )

5. People appearing before the court should wear business clothing. (   )

6. Nobody should ever wear a hat in the court. (   )

7. Children are allowed into the court. (   )

8. People should address others by family names instead of first names. (   )

9. Interruption is not allowed when the judge is speaking, but acceptable for other non-legal professionals. (   )

10. In general, people must have permission to move beyond a certain point toward the judge or jury. (   )

II. Choose the proper words from the list below to fill in the blanks. Change the form of the words if necessary.

> process / contempt / permit / prepared / representative
> formal / affect / attire / disruptive / business

In the court all people's clothing and act matters much because improper ___1___ may well cause people to be cited for ___2___ of court. Besides, your appearance will also ___3___ the impression the court has on you. Anyone appearing in the court should have respect for the judge as a ___4___ of the court and respect for the courtroom ___5___. To show the respect, people are supposed to arrive early and ___6___. ___7___ clothing is the appropriate dress code and food or drinks is not allowed to bring into the court. ___8___ or noisy children should be taken out of the courtroom. Without ___9___, nobody should move beyond a certain point toward the judge or jury. About the language use in the court, people should use ___10___ and brief language to answer questions.

UNIT 8
LEGAL ETHICS

Legal **ethics** are an area of ethics which involve the legal profession and the practice of law. It is a term used to describe a **code of conduct** governing proper professional behavior, which establishes the nature of obligations owed to individuals and to society. **Adherence** to basic legal ethics is generally required for people who wish to practice law, with most nations having associations of legal professionals which have the ability to bring people up on charges and **suspend** their licenses if they are suspected of ethics **violations.** For people seeking legal assistance who are curious, it is usually possible to look a lawyer up with a bar association to determine whether or not the lawyer is a member in good standing and to see a history of any complaints or investigations.

The practice of law is complex, and it can be **fraught** with ethical issues. Legal ethics covers many of the basic ethical issues which come up in the law, many of which are actually encoded right into the laws which **pertain** to legal practice. The goal of creating ethical standards is to retain the reputation of the legal profession as a whole, giving consumers greater confidence when it comes to dealing with lawyers. In order to maintain a license to practice law, attorneys in the United States agree to uphold the Rules of Professional Conduct, adopted by the American Bar Association (ABA) in 1983. The ABA's rules have been adopted by the bar associations of all the states except California, which has a similar code but with a different format.

Some topics covered in legal ethics include attorney-client **privilege**, legal **billing**, **disclosures** which lawyers are obligated to make, professional and personal relationships with other members of the legal profession, relationships with jurors, situations in which lawyers and judges must be **recused** from a case, ethical conflicts which can arise in the law, and situations in which people can offer legal advice. In many nations, legal ethics also include **mandates** to perform volunteer service, or a strong stress on performing **pro bono** work.

Advertising activities are also covered under legal ethics, as are the operations of legal firms, partnerships of attorneys, and so forth. When lawyers apply to be allowed to practice law, they are often required to swear or **affirm** an **oath** which indicates their intention to abide by ethical requirements, and they **subject** themselves **to** the authority of a government organization which has the power to enact **fines**, **revoke** licenses, and engage in other **penal** activities when ethical violations occur.

The field of legal ethics is constantly evolving as new legal issues arise. Many law schools have ethics committees and departments which explore shifts in legal ethics, as do professional associations of lawyers. These organizations may **periodically** recommend revisions or **alterations** to ethical guidelines in the interests of keeping members of the legal profession as current with ethical issues as possible.

New Words & Expressions

ethics	[ˈeθɪks]	n.	伦理，道德；伦理学
code of conduct			行为准则；规范
adherence	[ədˈhɪərəns]	n.	坚持，依附
suspend	[səˈspend]	vi. &vt.	延缓，推迟；使暂停
violation	[ˌvaɪəˈleɪʃn]	n.	违反，妨碍，侵犯
fraught	[frɔːt]	adj.	担心的，忧虑的；充满……的
pertain	[pəˈteɪn]	vi.	属于，关于
privilege	[ˈprɪvəlɪdʒ]	n.	特权，优待
billing	[ˈbɪlɪŋ]	n.	收费，开出账单
disclosure	[dɪsˈkləʊzə(r)]	n.	披露，揭发
recuse	[rɪˈkjuːz]	vt.	要求撤换

UNIT 8
LEGAL ETHICS

mandate	['mændeɪt]	n.	授权,命令;
		vt.	授权,托管;
pro bono	[ˌprəʊ 'bəʊnəʊ]	adj.	无偿的,公益的
affirm	[ə'fɜːm]	vi. &vt.	肯定,确认
oath	[əʊθ]	n.	誓言,誓约
subject to			使服从;受……管制
fine	[faɪn]	n.	付款
revoke	[rɪ'vəʊk]	vt.	撤回,取消,废除
penal	['piːnl]	adj.	刑事的,刑罚的
periodically	[ˌpɪərɪ'ɒdɪklɪ]	adv.	定期的,周期性的
alteration	[ˌɔːltə'reɪʃn]	n.	修改,改变

Exercises

I. Judge whether the statements below are true (T) or false (F).

1. Legal ethics define the code of conduct governing legal professionals. (   )

2. Even if legal professionals violate legal ethics, they will not be taken away their license. (   )

3. The practice of law is complex, but it seldom involves ethical issues. (   )

4. The goal of creating ethical standards is to give lawyers greater confidence when it comes to dealing with ethical issues. (   )

5. Legal ethics help retain the reputation of the legal profession as a whole. (   )

6. In all countries, performing pro bono work is an important part of legal ethics. (   )

7. The ABA's rules have been adopted by the bar associations of all U.S. states. (   )

8. When lawyers apply to be a licensed lawyer, they often have to swear an oath declaring to abide by ethical requirements. (   )

9. Only government organizations can recommend revisions of ethical guidelines. (   )

10. The goal of revisions or alterations to ethical guidelines is to update members of the legal profession the current ethical issues. (   )

II. Translate the following paragraph about legal ethics into Chinese.

The practice of law is complex, and it can be fraught with ethical issues. Legal ethics are the code of conduct governing proper professional behavior. Adherence to basic legal professional ethics is generally required for people who wish to practice law and legal professionals may get their licenses suspended if they are suspected of ethics violations. As new legal issues arise, many law schools and professional associations of lawyers may periodically recommend revisions or alterations to ethical guidelines in the interests of keeping members of the legal profession as current with professional ethical issues as possible.

UNIT 9
CHIEF JUSTICE IN THE UNITED STATES

Often incorrectly called the "**Chief Justice** of the Supreme Court," the Chief Justice of the United States not only presides over the Supreme Court, he or she serves as the head of the judicial branch of the federal government. The other eight members of the Supreme Court are called "**Associate Justices** of the Supreme Court."

The Chief Justice serves as the head of the Judicial Conference of the United States, the chief administrative body of the United States federal courts. The Judicial Conference is **empowered** by the Rules Enabling Act to **promulgate** rules to ensure the smooth operation of the federal courts. The Chief Justice presides over the Court's public sessions and also presides over the Court's private conferences, where the justices decide what cases to hear and how to vote on the cases they have heard.

Just like the **Associate Justices**, the Chief Justice of the United States is nominated by the President of the United States and must be confirmed by a majority vote of the U.S. Senate. Also like the Associate Justices, the Chief Justice serves until retirement, death or **impeachment**. The Chief Justice is also paid more than the Associate Justices.

The duties of the Chief Justice of the United States are not **elaborated** in the Constitution; instead, they have been **devised** and clarified over the years by Congress and the federal judiciary. In addition to the duties of the Associate Justices, the Chief Justice enters the courtroom first and casts the first vote when the justices **deliberate**. However, the Chief Justice's vote carries no more influence than the votes of the Associate Justices. If the Chief Justice votes with the majority in a case decided by the Supreme Court, he or she may choose to write the Court's opinion, or to assign the task to one of the Associate Justices. The Chief Justice sits as the judge in impeachments of the President of the United States. Only two Chief Justices have ever served this role: Chief Justices, Salmon P. Chase presided over the Senate trial of President Andrew Johnson in 1868, and the late William H. Rehnquist presided over the trial of President William Clinton in 1999.The Chief Justice swears in the President of the United States at **inaugurations**. This is a purely traditional role. According to law, any federal or state judge, even a **notary-public**, is empowered to administer oaths of office. The Chief Justice writes an **annual** report to Congress about the state of the federal court system.

As of March 2016, there have been 17 Chief Justices throughout the history of the United States. One of the most influential Chief Justices of the Supreme Court of the United States is John Marshall because court opinions helped lay the basis for United States constitutional law and many say made the Supreme Court of the United States a coequal branch of government along with the legislative and executive branches. He was also the longest-serving Chief Justice and the fourth longest-serving justice in U.S. Supreme Court history. Marshall dominated the Court for over three decades and played a significant role in the development of the American legal system. Most notably, he reinforced the principle that federal courts are obligated to exercise judicial review, by disregarding purported laws if they violate the constitution. Thus, Marshall cemented the position of the American judiciary as an independent and influential branch of government.

New Words & Expressions

the Chief Justice			首席大法官
the Associate Justices			（美国最高法院的）大法官
empower	[ɪmˈpaʊə(r)]	vt.	授权，允许
promulgate	[ˈprɒmlgeɪt]	vt.	公布，颁布
impeachment	[ɪmˈpiːtʃmənt]	n.	弹劾，控告
elaborate	[ɪˈlæbərət]	vi.&vt.	详细叙述

UNIT 9
CHIEF JUSTICE IN THE UNITED STATES

devise	[dɪˈvaɪz]	vt.	设计，想出
deliberate	[dɪˈlɪbərət]	vi.&vt.	仔细考虑
Inauguration	[ɪˌnɔːgjəˈreɪʃn]	n.	就职典礼
notary-public	[ˈnəʊtərɪ ˈpʌblɪk]	n.	公证人，公证员
annual	[ˈænjuəl]	adj.	年度的，一年一次的；
		n.	年刊

Exercises

I. Judge whether the statements below are true (T) or false (F).

1. Besides the Chief Justice, there are eight Associate Justices in the Supreme Court. (   )

2. The Chief Justice of the United States can only presides over the Supreme Court. (   )

3. The duties of the Chief Justice of the United States are elaborated clearly in the Constitution. (   )

4. The Chief Justice and the Associate Justices shall preside together over the Senate during any impeachment trial of the President. (   )

5. The Chief Justice and the Associate Justices are all nominated and confirmed by the U. S. President. (   )

6. The Chief Justice serves longer than the Associate Justices and are also paid more than the Associate Justices. (   )

7. The Chief Justice's greatest power is to decide who writes the Court's majority opinion if, but only if, the Chief Justice has voted with the majority. (   )

8. The Chief Justice's vote carries more influence than the votes of the Associate Justices. (   )

9. John Marshall, the first Chief Justice in the history of the United States, helped lay the basis for United States constitutional law. (   )

10. John Marshall was the longest-serving Chief Justice and the fourth longest-serving justice in U.S. Supreme Court history. (   )

II. Translate the following duties of the Chief Justice in the U. S. Supreme Court into Chinese.

1. The Chief Justice enters the courtroom first and casts the first vote when the justices deliberate. The Chief Justice's vote carries no more influence than the votes of the Associate Justices.
2. If the Chief Justice votes with the majority in a case decided by the Supreme Court, he or she may choose to write the Court's opinion, or to assign the task to one of the Associate Justices.
3. The Chief Justice sits as the judge in impeachments of the President of the United States.
4. The Chief Justice swears in the President of the United States at inaugurations. This is a purely traditional role.
5. The Chief Justice writes an annual report to Congress about the state of the federal court system.

UNIT 10
LAWYERS

The legal system affects nearly every aspect of our society, from buying a home to crossing the street. Lawyers form the **backbone** of this system, linking it to society in numerous ways. Lawyers, also called attorneys, act as both **advocates** and advisors in our society. As advocates, they represent one of the **parties** in criminal and civil trials by presenting evidence and arguing in court to support their client. As advisors, lawyers **counsel** their clients about their legal rights and obligations and suggest particular courses of action in business and personal matters.

The more detailed aspects of a lawyer's job depend upon his or her field of specialization and position. Although all lawyers are licensed to represent parties in court, some appear in court more frequently than others. **Trial lawyers** spend the majority of their time outside the courtroom, conducting research, interviewing clients and witnesses, and handling other details in preparation for a trial.

Lawyers may specialize in a number of areas, such as bankruptcy, **probate**, international, elder, or environmental law. These lawyers help clients prepare and **file** for licenses and applications for approval before certain activities are permitted to occur. Or they advise insurance companies about the legality of **transactions**, guiding the company in writing policies to **conform** to the law and to protect the companies from **unwarranted** claims. Most lawyers are in **private practice**, concentrating on criminal or civil law. In criminal law, lawyers represent individuals who have been charged with crimes and argue their cases in courts of law. Attorneys dealing with civil law assist clients with litigation, wills, **trusts**, contracts, **mortgages**, titles, and **leases**. Other lawyers handle only public-interest cases—civil or criminal—concentrating on particular causes and choosing cases that might have an impact on the way law is applied. Lawyers sometimes are employed full time by a single client. If the client is a corporation, the lawyer is known as "**house counsel**" and usually advises the company concerning legal issues related to its business activities. These issues might involve patents, government regulations, contracts with other companies, **property interests**, or **collective-bargaining agreements** with unions.

A significant number of attorneys are employed at the various levels of government. Some work for State attorneys general, prosecutors, and public defenders in criminal courts. At the Federal level, attorneys investigate cases for the U.S. Department of Justice and other agencies. Government lawyers also help develop programs, draft and interpret laws and legislation, establish **enforcement** procedures, and argue civil and criminal cases on behalf of the government. Other lawyers work for legal aid societies—private, nonprofit organizations established to serve disadvantaged people. These lawyers generally handle civil, rather than criminal, cases.

Lawyers do most of their work in offices, law libraries, and courtrooms. They sometimes meet in clients' homes or places of business and, when necessary, in hospitals or prisons. They may travel to attend meetings, gather evidence, and appear before courts, legislative bodies, and other authorities. They also may face particularly heavy pressure when a case is being tried. Lawyers often work long hours; of those who work full time, about 33 percent work 50 or more hours per week.

New Words & Expressions

backbone	[ˈbækbəʊn]	n.	支柱, 骨干
advocate	[ˈædvəkeɪt]	n.	代讼人
party	[ˈpɑːtɪ]	n.	当事人
counsel	[ˈkaʊnsl]	vt.	提出(法律)建议, 忠告
trial lawyer	[ˈtraɪəl ˈlɔːjə(r)]		出庭辩护的律师

probate	[ˈprəʊbeɪt]	vt.	遗嘱认证
		n.	遗嘱检验；经认证的遗嘱
		adj.	（法）遗嘱认证的
file	[faɪl]	vi. &vt.	提起（申请等）
transaction	[trænˈzækʃn]	n.	交易
unwarranted	[ʌnˈwɒrəntɪd]	adj.	无根据的, 无保证的
conform	[kənˈfɔːm]	vi.&vt.	符合, 遵照；使符合
trust	[trʌst]	n.	信托, 基金
mortgage	[ˈmɔːgɪdʒ]	n.	抵押；抵押贷款
lease	[liːs]	n.	租约, 租赁权
house counsel			企业法律顾问, 公司专职法律顾问
property interests			财产利益
collective-bargaining agreements			劳资协议
enforcement	[ɪnˈfɔːsmənt]	n.	执行, 实施
private practice			（律师）私人辩护, 私营辩护

Exercises

I. Judge whether the statements below are true (T) or false (F).

1. Lawyers, also called attorneys, act either as advocates or advisors in our society.
( )

2. Lawyers represent one of the parties in criminal and civil trials by presenting evidence and arguing in court to support their client. ( )

3. As advisors, lawyers do not have to research the intent of laws and judicial decisions faced by their clients. ( )

4. Trial lawyers spend the majority of their time in the courtroom presenting evidence and very little time outside the courtroom to prepare for a trial.( )

5. It is possible that lawyers specialize in a number of areas. ( )

6. Very few lawyers are in private practice, and most of them handle only public-interest cases. (   )

7. House counsels advise the company concerning legal issues related to its business activities. (   )

8. Lawyers working for legal aid societies generally handle civil, rather than criminal, cases. (   )

9. According to professional ethics, lawyers cannot meet in clients' homes but in public venues. (   )

10. Lawyers cannot work over 50 hours per week according to the passage. (   )

II. Choose appropriate words to finish the passage below about the lawyers' responsibilities. Change the form of the words if necessary.

> confer / advisor / counsel / enforcement / evidence
> conform / attorney / transaction / property / judicial

Lawyers, also called ___1___ , form the backbone of the social system and bear great responsibilities. When lawyers act as advocates, they present ___2___ and argue in court for their clients. Besides, lawyers also work as ___3___ by ___4___ their clients about their legal rights and obligations. Lawyers may specialize in a number of areas, such as bankruptcy, probate, international or intellectual ___5___ law. Some lawyers advise companies about the legality of ___6___ , guiding the company in writing policies to ___7___ to the law and to protect the companies from unwarranted claims. Some lawyers work for the government and they help develop programs, draft and interpret laws and legislation, establish ___8___ procedures, and argue civil and criminal cases on behalf of the government. Lawyers may face particularly heavy pressure when a case is being tried when they prepare for court includes understanding the latest laws and ___9___ decisions. Lawyers in private practice may work irregular hours, while ___10___ with clients or preparing briefs during non-office hours.

UNIT 11
COMMON LAW & CIVIL LAW SYSTEM

Most nations today follow one of two major legal systems: common law or civil law. The common law tradition emerged in England during the Middle Ages and was applied within British colonies across continents. It is still being used in Australia, most of Canada, England, India and the United States. The civil law tradition developed in continental Europe at the same time and was applied in the colonies of European imperial powers such as Spain and Portugal. Civil law was also adopted in the nineteenth and twentieth centuries by countries formerly possessing distinctive legal traditions, such as Russia and Japan, which sought to reform their legal systems in order to gain economic and political power comparable to that of Western European nation-states.

Even though England had many profound cultural ties to the rest of Europe in the Middle Ages, its legal tradition developed differently from that of the continent for a number of historical reasons, and one of the most fundamental ways in which they diverged was in the establishment of judicial decisions as the basis of common law and legislative decisions as the basis of civil law.

Common Law

Common law is generally **uncodified**. This means that there is no comprehensive **compilation** of legal rules and statutes. While common law does rely on some scattered statutes, which are legislative decisions, it is largely based on **precedents**, meaning the judicial decisions that have already been made in similar cases. These precedents are maintained over time through the records of the courts as well as historically documented in collections of case law known as yearbooks and reports. The precedents to be applied in the decision of each new case are determined by the **presiding judge**. As a result, judges have an enormous role in shaping American and British law. Common law functions as an **adversarial** system, a contest between two opposing parties before a judge who moderates. A **jury of** ordinary people without legal training decides on the facts of the case. The judge then determines the appropriate sentence based on the jury's **verdict.**

Civil Law

Civil law, in contrast, is codified. Countries with civil law systems have comprehensive, continuously updated legal codes that specify all matters capable of being brought before a court, the applicable procedure, and the appropriate punishment for each **offense**. Such codes distinguish between different categories of law: **substantive law** establishes which acts are subject to criminal or civil prosecution, procedural law establishes how to determine whether a particular action constitutes a criminal act, and **penal law** establishes the appropriate penalty. In a civil law system, the judge takes on an inquisitional role to establish the facts of the case by asking the parties questions and to apply the provisions of the applicable code. Though the judge often brings the formal charges, investigates the matter, and decides on the case, he or she works within a framework established by a comprehensive, codified set of laws. The judge's decision is consequently less crucial in shaping civil law than the decisions of legislators and legal scholars who draft and interpret the codes

Historical Development of Common Law

Common law emerged from the changing and centralizing powers of the king in England during the Middle Ages. After the Norman Conquest in 1066, medieval kings began to consolidate power and establish new institutions of royal authority and justice. New forms of legal action established by the crown functioned through a system of **writs**, or royal orders, each of which provided a specific remedy for a specific wrong. The system of writs became so highly formalized that the laws the courts could apply based on this system often were too rigid to adequately achieve justice. In these cases, a further appeal to justice would have to be made directly to the king. This difficulty gave birth to a new kind of court, **the court of equity**, also known as the court of **Chancery** because it was the court of the king's chancellor. Courts of equity were authorized to apply principles of equity based on many sources (such as Roman law and natural law) rather than to apply only the common law, to achieve a just outcome.

Courts of law and courts of equity thus functioned separately until the writs system was abolished in the mid-nineteenth century. Even today, however, some U.S. states maintain separate courts of equity. Likewise, certain kinds of writs, such as warrants and **subpoenas**, still exist in the modern practice of common law. An example is the writ of **habeas corpus**, which protects the individual from unlawful detention. Originally an order from the king obtained by a prisoner or on his behalf, a writ of habeas corpus summoned the prisoner to court to determine whether he was being detained under lawful authority.

Civil Law Influences in American Law

The American legal system remains firmly within the common law tradition brought to the North American colonies from England. Yet traces of the civil law tradition and its importance in the hemisphere maybe found within state legal traditions across the United States. Most prominent is the example of Louisiana, where state law is based on civil law as a result of Louisiana's history as a French and Spanish territory prior to its purchase from France in 1803. Many of the southwestern states reflect traces of civil law influence in their state constitutions and codes from their early legal heritage as territories of colonial Spain and Mexico. California, for instance, has a state civil code organized into sections that echo traditional Roman civil law categories **pertaining** to persons, things, and actions; yet the law contained within California's code is mostly common law.

New Words & Expressions

uncodified	[ˈkɒdɪˌfaɪd]	adj.	未编成法典的
compilation	[ˌkɒmpɪˈleɪʃn]	n.	编译，编辑，汇编
precedent	[ˈpresɪdənt]	n.	先例

UNIT 11
COMMON LAW & CIVIL LAW SYSTEM

presiding judge			审判长, 首席法官, 法庭庭长
adversarial	[ˌædvəˈseərɪəl]	*adj.*	对抗的; 对手的, 敌手的
jury	[ˈdʒʊərɪ]	*n.*	陪审团
verdict	[ˈvɜːdɪkt]	*n.*	结论; 裁定
offense	[əˈfens]	*n.*	犯罪, 过错
substantive law			实体法
penal law			刑法
writ	[rɪt]	*n.*	令状
the court of equity			衡平法庭
Chancery	[ˈtʃɑːnsərɪ]	*n.*	(英) 大法官法庭
subpoena	[səˈpiːnə]	*n.*	传票
		vt.	传唤, 传审; 传讯
habeas corpus			人身保护令
pertaining to			与……有关

Exercises

I. Complete the following chart about the differences between the common law and civil law with the information you've got from the passage.

	common law	civil law
History	It have evolved primarily in _____ and its former _____, including Australia, Canada, England, India and the United States.	It developed in _____ at the same time and was applied in the colonies of _____ such as Spain and Portugal.

43

Legal system	Legal system is largely based on _____, which is _____ that have already been made in similar cases.	Legal system originating in Europe whose primary source of law is _____ that specify all matters capable of being brought before a court.
Roles of judges	Judges make laws. They _____ between lawyers and determines _____ based on the jury's _____.	The judge takes on an _____ role to establish _____ by asking the parties questions and to apply the provisions of _____. Its decisions are not the major source of civil law.
Types of argument in the court	_____: a contest between two opposing parties before a judge.	Inquisitorial: judges, not lawyers, ask questions and demand evidence.
Jury	A jury of _____ decides on _____.	

II. Choose the best answer for each of the following questions.

1. What is the major characteristic of civil law system that distinguishes it from the common law system?

    A. It is based on the judicial precedents.

    B. It is based on the legal codes.

    C. Judges make laws.

    D. It has an adversarial system.

2. What does "verdict" mean?

   A. the findings of a jury on issues of fact submitted to it for decision

   B. the punishment imposed upon the defendant following a conviction in a criminal proceeding

   C. a commitment to tell the truth

   D. the confirmation of a voidable act

3. What is procedural law?

   A. It establishes which acts are subject to criminal or civil prosecution.

   B. It establishes the appropriate penalty.

   C. It regulates the legal relationships between individuals and the government.

   D. It establishes how to determine whether a particular action constitutes a criminal act.

4. In the civil law system, who plays a major role in making the civil law?

   A. the judges

   B. the jurors

   C. the legislators

   D. the scholars

5. What is the earliest common law?

   A. The writs

   B. Natural law

   C. Roman law

   D. Equity law

6. Which of the following statements is not true about the court of equity?

   A. The court of equity was established because the writs system is too rigid to adequately achieve justice.

   B. It was the court of the king's chancellor.

   C. It was authorized to apply only the common law.

   D. Some U.S. states still maintain separate courts of equity.

7. What is the writ of habeas corpus?

   A. a writ that states that a person cannot be kept in prison unless they have first been brought before a court of law, which decides whether it is legal for them to be kept in prison

   B. a writ issued by court authority to compel the attendance of a witness at a judicial proceeding

   C. a writ from a court the police permission to arrest someone or search their house

   D. a writ directing the sheriff to seize the property

8. All of the States in United States adopt the common law system EXCEPT the state of _____.

   A. California

   B. Louisiana

   C. Texas

   D. Minnesota

UNIT 12
JURY TRIAL

A **jury trial** or trial by jury is a legal proceeding in which a jury either makes a decision or makes findings of fact, which then direct the actions of a judge. It is distinguished from a **bench trial**, in which a judge or panel of judges make all decisions.

Jury trials are used in a significant share of serious criminal cases in almost all common law legal systems, and juries or lay judges have been incorporated into the legal systems of many civil law countries for criminal cases. Only the United States makes routine use of jury trials in a wide variety of non-criminal cases. Other common law legal jurisdictions use jury trials only in a very select class of cases that make up a tiny share of the overall civil docket (e.g. defamation suits in England and Wales), while true civil jury trials are almost entirely absent elsewhere in the world. Some civil law jurisdictions do, however, have arbitration panels where non-legally trained members decide cases in select subject-matter areas relevant to the **arbitration** panel members' areas of expertise.

Before the process of hearing any testimony during trial, jury selection is the most important preliminary part of any criminal trial because many attorneys believe that trials are won or lost on the basis of which jurors are selected. The process of choosing a jury is a combination of random selection through the jury pool selection process and the juror elimination process performed by the lawyers for each side. There are three important stages in jury selection: compiling a master list, summoning the venire, and conducting **voir dire.**

> For most courts, the creation of the master jury list is the first critical step in the jury selection process. The important goal of this step is to make a list that

is broadly inclusive of the jury—**eligible** people who are **geographically** and **demographically** representative of the community.

➤ Venire is the second important step in jury selection. The venire is a group of citizens from which jury members are chosen (jury pool). Generally, the person or **jury commissioner** who works at court decides how many jurors to call for a given trial. Then, the names of jury members are **randomly** chosen from the master jury list.

➤ The last step in jury selection is voir dire. Voir dire is a preliminary examination of prospective jurors in order to determine their qualifications to serve as jurors. The judge may ask questions, although the lawyers for both parties will do that primarily.

The availability of a trial by jury in American jurisdictions varies. Because the United States legal system separated from that of the English at the time of the American Revolution, the types of proceedings that use juries depends on whether such cases were tried by jury under English common law at that time, rather than the methods used in English or UK courts in the present. For example, at the time English "courts of law" tried cases of torts or private law for monetary damages but "courts of equity" tried civil cases seeking an injunction or another form of non-monetary relief. As a result, this practice continues in American civil laws, even though in modern English law only criminal proceedings and some **inquests** are likely to be heard by a jury.

The use of jury trials evolved within common law systems rather than civil law systems has had a profound impact on the nature of American civil procedure and criminal procedure rules, even in cases where a bench trial is actually contemplated in a particular case. In general, the availability of a jury trial if properly demanded has given rise to a system where fact finding is concentrated in a single trial rather than multiple hearings, and where appellate review of trial court decisions is greatly limited. Jury trials are of far less importance (or of no importance) in countries that do not have a common law system.

UNIT 12
JURY TRIAL

In the United States, every person accused of a crime punishable **by incarceration** for more than six months has a constitutional right to a trial by jury, which arises in federal court from Article Three of the United States Constitution, which states in part, "The Trial of all Crimes...shall be by Jury; and such Trial shall be held in the State where the said Crimes shall have been committed." The right was expanded with the Sixth Amendment to the United States Constitution, which states in part, "In all criminal prosecutions, the accused shall enjoy the right to a speedy and public trial, by an impartial jury of the state and district wherein the crime shall have been committed." Both provisions were made applicable to the states through the Fourteenth Amendment. Most states' constitutions also grant the right of trial by jury in lesser criminal matters, though most have abrogated that right in offenses punishable by fine only. The Supreme Court has ruled that if **imprisonment** is for six months or less, trial by jury is not required, meaning a state may choose whether or not to permit trial by jury in such cases. Under the Federal Rules of Criminal Procedure, if the defendant is entitled to a jury trial, he may **waive** his right to have a jury, but both the government (prosecution) and court must consent to the waiver. Several states require jury trials for all crimes, "petty" or not.

New Words & Expressions

jury trial			陪审团审判
bench trial			法官审判
arbitration	[ˌɑːbɪˈtreɪʃn]	n.	仲裁，公断
voir dire		n.	一切照实陈述（见证人或陪审员在接受审核时的誓语）
eligible	[ˈelɪdʒəbl]	adj.	合格的，合适的；符合条件的；有资格当选的
geographically	[ˌdʒiːəˈɡræfɪklɪ]	adv.	地理学上，在地理上，地理方面
demographically	[diːməˈtɪərɪəlaɪz]	adv.	人口统计地
jury commissioner			陪审团审查官

randomly	['rændəmlɪ]	adv.	随便地，未加计划地
inquest	['ɪŋkwest]	n.	〈法〉(有陪审员列席的)审讯；验尸；查询，调查；公审庭，陪审团
incarceration	[ɪnˌkɑːsə'reɪʃn]	n.	监禁，禁闭；钳闭
imprisonment	[ɪm'prɪznmənt]	n.	关押，监禁；"imprison"的派生
waive	[weɪv]	vt.	宣布放弃；搁置；推迟；放弃(权利、要求等)

Exercises

I. Choose the best answer for each of the following questions.

1. A jury is _____.

    A. a group of professional lawyers serving temporarily in the court

    B. a group of normal laypersons serving temporarily in the court

    C. an institution composed of lawyers serving in a two-year term

    D. an institution composed of laypersons serving in a two-year term

2. Which of the following people is Not eligible for jury service?

    A. An American citizen

    B. An 18-year-old student

    C. A person with a clear criminal background

    D. A person with mental problems

3. What does "venire" mean?

    A. a group of people summoned for jury service, from whom a jury will be chosen

    B. a conduct that makes another person suffer but does not involve physical assault

    C. a warrant authorizing the taking into custody of a person who has fled from one state to another to avoid prosecution or punishment for crime

    D. a statement that denies something, especially responsibility

4. Which of the following statements about jury duty is NOT true?

    A. Inability to speak and read English can be excused from jury duty.

UNIT 12
JURY TRIAL

   B. firefighters can be excused from jury summon because their time was much too valuable to spend on jury duty.

   C. The elimination of statutory exemptions indicates the significance of the jury duty.

   D. The failure to meet one's jury duty is common and acceptable in most of states.

5. What is "Voir Dire"?

   A. It refers to a discrepancy between two statements or documents.

   B. It refers to a writ summoning prospective jurors.

   C. It refers to the process by which prospective jurors are questioned by the attorneys and/or the judge to determine their qualifications to serve as jurors

   D. It refers to the process by which a person is summoned to act as a juror from among the bystanders in a court.

II. Choose the proper words from the list below to fill in the blanks. Change the form of the words if necessary.

> instruction / innocent / involved / witness / observe
> represent / guarantee / verdict / institution / accused

The American Jury system began in England and then spread to some other countries in Europe and Anglo Saxon countries. The jury system became a remarkable ____1____ for educating people about the law in their country. The jury consists of fair-minded citizens who ____2____ their local community. During the trial, the juries ____3____ obscure or contested evidence which helps them make a decision. They receive legal ____4____ from the judge. They also listen to people ____5____ in the trial. Then jurors go into a room alone to decide a ____6____ without any help from any experts. Their task is to judge the facts of the case and decide the significance of the evidence and credibility of ____7____ to determine the truth. Their decisions will be to decide whether the _____8_____ person is either guilty or _____9_____. Fairness and justice is shaped in trial by a jury which is the only _____10_____ against the power of government, corruption of officials, prejudice of appointed judges and the bureaucracy of applying legal rules.

UNIT 13
COURT SYSTEM IN THE UNITED STATES

Courts in the United States are organized two distinct systems: the federal courts and the state courts. Although created under separate governments, the methods of operation and organization of these two systems are similar.

Federal Courts

The Supreme Court of the United States is the highest court in the federal system. The courts of **appeals** are **intermediate** courts. The district courts and special courts are the lower courts

- **Supreme Court.** The Supreme Court is the only federal court expressly established by the Constitution. Congress is authorized by the Constitution to create other federal courts.

    The Supreme Court has original **jurisdiction** in all cases affecting ambassadors, other public ministers, and **consuls**, and in those cases in which a state is a party. Except as regulated by Congress, it has **appellate** jurisdiction in all cases that may be brought into the federal courts in accordance with the terms of the Constitution. The Supreme Court also has appellate jurisdiction of certain cases that have been decided by the supreme courts of the states. Thousands of cases are **filed** with this court in a year.

- **Courts of Appeals.** The United States, including the District of Columbia, is divided into 12 **judicial circuits**. Each of the circuits has a court of appeals. These courts are courts of record.

    A court of appeals has appellate jurisdiction only and is empowered to review the final decisions of the district courts, except in cases that may be taken directly to the Supreme Court. The decisions of the courts of appeals are final in most cases. An appeal may be taken on certain constitutional questions. Otherwise, review depends on the **discretion** of the Supreme Court and, in some cases, of the court of appeals.

- **District Courts.** The United States, including the District of Columbia, is divided into a number of judicial districts. Some states form a single district, whereas others are divided into two or more districts. District courts are also located in the **territories**. The district courts have original jurisdiction in practically all cases that may be maintained in the federal courts. They are the trial courts for civil and criminal cases.

- **Other Federal Courts.** In addition to the Supreme Court, the Courts of appeals, and the district courts, the following tribunals have been created by Congress to determine other matters as indicated by their titles: Court of International Trade, **Claims Court**, Tax Court, Court of Military Appeals, and the territorial Courts.

State Courts

Court system in the various states is organized along lines similar to the federal court system, although differing in details, such as the number of courts, their names, and jurisdiction.

- **State Supreme Court.** The highest court in most states is known as the Supreme Court. In a few states it may have a different name, such as "Court of Appeals" in New York. The jurisdiction of a supreme court is ordinarily appellate, although in a few instances it is original. In some states the Supreme Court is required to **render** an opinion on certain questions that may be referred to by the legislature or by the chief executive of the state. The decision of a state Supreme Court is final in all cases not involving the federal Constitution, laws, and treaties.

- **Intermediate Courts.** In some states, intermediate courts have original jurisdiction in a few cases but, in the main, they have appellate jurisdiction of

UNIT 13
COURT SYSTEM IN THE UNITED STATES

cases removed for **review** from the county or district courts. They are known as superior, circuit, or district appellate courts. As a general rule, their decisions may be reviewed by the highest state court.

➤ **County and District Courts.** These courts of record have appellate jurisdiction of cases tried in the justice of the peace and police courts, as well as general original jurisdiction of criminal and civil cases. They also have jurisdiction of wills and guardianship matters, except when, as in some states, the jurisdiction of such cases has been given to special orphans', **surrogate**, or **probate** courts

➤ **Other State Courts.** In addition to the foregoing, the following, which are ordinarily not courts of record, have jurisdiction as indicated by their titles: city or municipal courts, police courts, traffic courts, small claims courts, and justice of the peace courts.

New Words & Expressions

appeal	[əˈpiːl]	vi.	呼吁，恳求；上诉
		n.	呼吁，请求；上诉
		vt.	将……上诉
intermediate	[ˌɪntəˈmiːdiət]	adj.	中级的
jurisdiction	[ˌdʒʊərɪsˈdɪkʃn]	n.	司法权，审判权，管辖权
consul	[ˈkɒnsl]	n.	领事
appellate	[əˈpelɪt]	adj.	上诉的；受理上诉的
file	[faɪl]	v.	提起（申请、诉讼等）
judicial circuit			巡回法院
discretion	[dɪˈskreʃn]	n.	自由裁量权
territory	[ˈterətri]	n.	领域，范围
Claims Court			索赔法院
render	[ˈrendə(r)]	vt.	做出（判决）；执行；实施

review	[rɪ'vju:]	n.	再审，复审
		vt.	再审，复审
surrogate court			遗嘱认证法院
probate court			遗嘱认证法院

Exercises

I. Choose the proper words from the list below to fill in the blanks. Change the form of the words if necessary.

> file / judicial / authorize / render / jurisdiction
> review / appeal / regulate / decision / discretion

1. The court has no _____ over cases of this kind.

2. The third party with an independent claim has the right to _____ a lawsuit against the subject disputed by the plaintiff and the defendant.

3. She said that she was trying to recover her property through legal means, but "so far, no judge has dared to _____ our complaint."

4. The right of individuals to _____ to a higher court is provided for in the constitution.

5. The _____ of the court bears on or has a bearing on future cases where immigration procedures are disputed.

6. The United Nations will approve his request for _____ the use of military force to deliver aid.

7. The old encoded rule may require _____ adaptation to meet changed conditions.

8. Not every violation of law can be prosecuted, and prosecutors have wide _____ in deciding which to prosecute and which to drop.

9. Juries nearly always _____ verdicts with which I agree.

10. The new treaty is designed to follow the Kyoto protocol, the world's existing treaty to _____ greenhouse gases, the first phase of which expires in 2012.

II. Translate the following phrases into English.

1. 下级法院　2. 最高法院　3. 上诉法院　4. 地方法院　5. 巡回法院
6. 初审法院　7. 中级法院　8. 初审管辖权　9. 民事案件　10. 刑事案件

III. Translate the following passage into Chinese.

The courts interpret the law. They also settle disagreements between individuals and the government. Different levels of courts handle different kinds of cases. Federal courts handle cases about the Constitution and the laws made by Congress. They also deal with problems between one or more states. The Supreme Court is the highest court in the judicial branch. The judges on the Supreme Court are called justices. The head of the Supreme Court is the Chief Justice. The Framers of Constitution believed that if judges were elected by the people, they might favor some people over others. For this reason, judges are not elected. They are appointed to office. Judges on all federal courts are appointed by the President. However, the Senate must approve all the President's appointments. Judges serve in the judicial branch until they retire or die. They can also be impeached, tried, and removed from their positions, just like the President.

UNIT 14
SOURCES OF LAW IN THE UNITED STATES

According to Black's **Law Dictionary**, the term "source of law" refers to something that provides **authority** for legislation and for judicial decisions. In other words, "sources of law" refers to the body of rules which a judge will draw upon in deciding a case, and where these rules are to be found. In civil law systems, one has only to look at the appropriate code; but in common law systems one needs to look at legislation and at the decided cases that comprise judicial precedent. Generally speaking, the main sources of law in the United States, which exist at both state and federal levels, are:

➤ **Constitution**;
➤ Legislation embodied in statutes and administrative regulations;
➤ Court opinions (also called cases or judicial precedents);

Constitution

The United States federal Constitution is the **preeminent** source of law in its legal system, and all other rules, whether **promulgated** by a state and the federal government, must **comply with** its requirements. There are 50 states and each state also has its own constitution. A state's constitution may grant greater rights than those secured by the federal constitution, but because a state constitution is subordinate to the federal constitution, it cannot provide lesser rights than the federal constitution does. All of state's legal rules must comport with both the state and federal constitutions.

A constitution establishes a system of government and defines the boundaries of authority granted to the government. The U.S. Constitution created three branches of government: the **legislative** branch, which makes the laws; the **judicial** branch, which interprets the laws; and the **executive** branch, which enforces the laws. The state constitution also establishes its distinct system of local government—its own legislative body, courts and executive branch. These three branches of government operate as a "check and balance" to prevent any singular branch from gaining too much power.

Legislation Embodied in Statutes and Administrative Regulations

Legislation is the prime source of law and consists in the declaration of legal rules by a competent authority. Legislation can have many purposes: to regulate, to authorize, to enable, to **proscribe**, to provide funds, to **sanction**, to grant, to declare or to restrict. Statutes are created by the legislative branch of government, which must be approved by the executive branch (the president, for federal statues; the governor, for state statues) to go into effect. The executive branch also makes rules or administrative regulations. Administrative agencies, such as **the federal Food and Drug Administration** or a state' **department of motor vehicles**, which are part of the executive branch, execute the laws passed by the legislature and create their own regulations to carry out the mandates established by statutes.

Court Opinions

Court opinion is judicial interpretation of the rules to the facts of a case. A public record of the court's decision is **filed** to **resolve** statutory interpretation and to guide future litigations. Court opinions can be an independent source of legal rules, **on equal footing with** statutes and regulations. Legal rules made by courts are called "common-law" rules, cases or judicial precedents. They are either binding on or persuasive for a court when deciding subsequent cases with similar issues or facts. The American legal system places great value on deciding cases according to consistent principled rules so that similar facts will yield similar and predictable outcomes, and **observance** of precedents is the mechanism by which that goal is attained. Although courts are **empowered** to make these rules, legislatures can adopt legislation that changes or **abolishes** a common-law rule, as long as the legislation is constitutional. And if a court determines that a rule does not meet constitutional requirements, it can **invalidate** the rule.

  These legal rules **enunciated** by each of the branches of government govern the conduct of society. Some legal works are another type of source of law in America. They are secondary source of law, persuasive but not blinding. When researching a legal issue, a legal practitioner is required to research several different types of legal authority. The answer to a research question may not be found exclusively in statutes or court opinions or administrative regulations. Often, these sources must be researched together to determine all of the rules applicable to factual scenario.

New Words & Expressions

authority	[ɔːˈθɒrəti]	n.	权威；法律依据
constitution	[ˌkɒnstɪˈtjuːʃn]	n.	宪法；体制；章程
preeminent	[priˈemɪnənt]	adj.	卓越的；优秀的；超群的
promulgate	[ˈprɒmlɡeɪt]	vt.	公布；传播；发表
comport with	[kəmˈpɔːt][wɪð]	v.	一致；适合
legislative	[ˈledʒɪslətɪv]	adj.	立法的；有立法权的
judicial	[dʒuˈdɪʃl]	adj.	司法的；法庭的；公正的；审判上的
executive	[ɪɡˈzekjətɪv]	adj.	行政的；决策的；经营的
statute	[ˈstætʃuːt]	n.	法令；法规；条例
proscribe	[prəˈskraɪb]	vt.	剥夺……的公权；禁止
sanction	[ˈsæŋkʃn]	n.	制裁，处罚；认可；支持
		vt.	制裁，处罚；批准；鼓励
the federal Food and Drug Administration			联邦食品和药物管理局
department of motor vehicles			车管所
mandate	[ˈmændeɪt]	n.	命令，指令
file	[faɪl]	vt.	提出；把……归档
resolve	[rɪˈzɒlv]	vt.	解决；决心要做……

UNIT 14
SOURCES OF LAW IN THE UNITED STATES

		vi.	解决；决心
on equal footing with...			与……同等地位
observance	[əbˈzɜːvəns]	n.	遵守
invalidate	[ɪnˈvælɪdeɪt]	vt.	使无效
empower	[ɪmˈpaʊə(r)]	vt.	授权；使能够
abolish	[əˈbɒlɪʃ]	vt.	废除；革除；消灭
enunciate	[ɪˈnʌnsɪeɪt]	vt.	阐明；宣布

Exercises

I. Match each legal term with its proper definition.

_____ 1. opinion a. relating to the legal system and to judgments made in a court of law

_____ 2. liability b. to deprive (an official document or procedure) of legal efficacy because of violation of a regulation or law

_____ 3. sanction c. a formal statement of reasons for a judgment given

_____ 4. litigation d. compulsory ; that must be obeyed because it is accepted in law

_____ 5. legislative e. the state of being legally obliged and responsible

_____ 6. statute f. to start legal proceedings against someone

_____ 7. binding g. official permission or approval for an action or a change

_____ 8. judicial h. the power or right to give orders or make decisions

_____ 9. sue i. having the power to make laws

_____ 10. invalidate j. the process of making or defending a claim in court

_____ 11. authority k. a written law passed by a legislative body

II. Complete the following figure with the information from the passage to show the relationships among the branches of government and types of legal rules they create.

UNINTED STATES CONSTITUTION

GOVERNMENT

STATE GOVERNMENT

Legislative Branch

(headed by the president)

Administrative Regulations (created by Administrative agencies pursuant To statutory authority)

Court Opinions (also called cases)

(headed by the governor)

Statutes

Administrative Regulations (created by administrative agencies pursuant to statutory authority)

Court Opinions (also called cases)

III. Judge whether the statements below are true (T) or false (F).

_____ 1. A state's constitution cannot provide greater rights than the federal constitution does because a state constitution is subordinate to the federal constitution.

_____ 2. The federal statutes created by Congress must be approved by the president.

_____ 3. Court can only interpret and apply rules to the cases. It has no power to invalidate any rules.

_____ 4. The president can change or abolish a common-law rule made by a court by adoption of a statute.

_____ 5. A state's department of motor vehicles can create administrative regulations to execute the statutes.

UNIT 15
SEVEN PRINCIPLES IN THE U.S. JUDICIAL SYSTEM

The United States is renowned for having one of the most sophisticated judicial systems in the world. Every day, thousands of people, including law enforcement officers, lawyers, judges, government officials and even **accused** criminals, take part in this system, hoping to settle disputes and work for justice. What makes this system even more remarkable is that it is able to operate successfully in a country as large and diverse as the United States. The keys to this success are the seven principles under which the judicial system of the United States operates:

> **The Rule of Law**

The rule of law is a concept which **embraces** a body of recognized or established principles, statutes, rules and regulations **to** which all citizens **are subject** and which are applied objectively by independent judges acting through established procedures. Under it the legal system is sufficiently separated from the political authority so that the rights under the law of citizens and other subjects to that authority will be **upheld** if they follow its rules.

> **Separation of Powers**

Separation of powers is a principle in which each of the three branches of government—the legislative branch, the executive branch, and the judicial branch—has separate and distinct responsibilities and functions. The legislative branch—the House of Representatives and the Senate, known collectively as Congress which is make up of representatives of citizens—creates and makes laws; the executive branch **enforces** these laws; and the judicial branch interprets the laws and applies them in cases and **controversies**.

> **Independent Judiciary**

Under this principle the judicial branch is free from outside influences of persons or institutions in the executive and legislative branches of government and from private persons and organizations. Judicial orders and decisions are made by judge on the basis of law, and the application of recognized and established legal principles and rules, and not on the basis of the **status** of the parties before the court or the **dictates** or influence of some person or agency within or without the government.

> **Judicial Review**

Judicial review is the right and the duty of a judge in a case or controversy to declare an act of the legislative or executive branch of the government **invalid** as being contrary to the constitution of the government under which the court operates or the duly **enacted** statutes of the legislative branch of that government.

> **Federalism**

Under this principle, two systems of government, including the judicial branch, coexist—one for the central government which is applicable to all states and their citizens equally, and one for each of the individual state which operates within the **geographical** boundaries of each of the individual states and to which citizens and others within those boundaries are subject. The successful operation of the U.S. judicial system in such a large and diverse country owes greatly to a balanced and carefully ordered hierarchy: Several different federal courts control issues relating to federal law and each state has its own set of courts that can adapt to the needs of its people.

> **Adversarial Process**

The U.S. legal system is in part inherited from English common law and depends on an adversarial system of justice. The adversarial process provides the means by which cases are presented in court. In this process lawyers completely and **vigorously** present evidence and legal arguments on behalf of their clients—the **litigants**—from which all of the facts and positions of a case are presented to the judge or jury so that a just decision can be rendered.

UNIT 15
SEVEN PRINCIPLES IN THE U.S. JUDICIAL SYSTEM

> **Due Process**

Due process is the legal requirement that the state must respect all legal rights that are owed to a person. When a government harms a person without following the exact course of the law, this constitutes a due process violation, which offends the rule of law. The requirement of due process guarantees to an individual who may be injured by, or suffer loss as a result of an act of government or the enforcement of legislation or other government decisions, the right to an institutional hearing to present the **grievance** and positions and arguments related to it, and to request **redress** of and **relief** from that grievance.

New Words & Expressions

accused	[əˈkjuːzd]	n.	被告
		adj.	被控告的
embrace	[ɪmˈbreɪs]	vt.	拥抱；信奉，皈依；包含
		vi.	拥抱
		n.	拥抱
be subject to			受支配，从属于；常遭受……；有……倾向的
uphold	[ʌpˈhəʊld]	vt.	支撑；鼓励；赞成；举起
enforce	[ɪnˈfɔːs]	vt.	实施，执行
controversy	[ˈkɒntrəvɜːsɪ]	n.	争论，争议
status	[ˈsteɪtəs]	n.	地位；身份
dictate	[dɪkˈteɪt]	vt.	命令；口述；使听写
		vi.	口述；听写
		n.	命令；指示
invalid	[ɪnˈvælɪd]	adj.	无效的
enact	[ɪˈnækt]	vt.	颁布；制定法律
federalism	[ˈfedərəlɪzəm]	n.	联邦制，联邦主义

geographical	[ˌdʒiːəˈgræfɪkl]	adj.	地理的
vigorously	[ˈvɪgərəsli]	adv.	充满力量地；强有力地
litigant	[ˈlɪtɪgənt]	n.	诉讼当事人
		adj.	诉讼的
due process			正当程序
grievance	[ˈgriːvəns]	n.	不满，不平；委屈；冤情
redress	[rɪˈdres]	vt.	救济；赔偿；纠正；重新调整
		n.	救济；赔偿；矫正
relief	[rɪˈliːf]	n.	救济

Exercises

I. Match each word with its proper definition.

_____ 1. regulations   a. a party to a lawsuit

_____ 2. enforce   b. to correct or to improve things for the person who has been badly treated

_____ 3. authority   c. to explain the meaning of sth.

_____ 4. evidence   d. involving people who are in opposition and who make attacks on each other

_____ 5. litigant   e. the right to command and control other people

_____ 6. enact   f. an allegation that something imposes an illegal obligation or denies some legal right or causes injustice

_____ 7. redress   g. to pass a law

_____ 8. grievance   h. to make sure that people obey a particular law or rule

_____ 9. interpret   i. the information that is used in a court of law to try to prove something

_____ 10. adversarial   j. rules made by a government or other authority in order to control the way something is done or the way people behave

II. Translate the following sentences into Chinese.

1. Separation of powers is a principle in which each of the three branches of government—the legislative branch, the executive branch, and the judicial branch—have separate and distinct responsibilities and functions.
2. Judicial orders and decisions are made by judge on the basis of law, and the application of recognized and established legal principles and rules, and not on the basis of the status of the parties before the court or the dictates or influence of some person or agency within or without the government.
3. In this process lawyers completely and vigorously present evidence and legal arguments on behalf of their clients—the litigants—from which all of the facts and positions of a case are presented to the judge or jury so that a just decision can be rendered
4. The requirement of due process guarantees to an individual who may be injured by, or suffer loss as a result of an act of government or the enforcement of legislation or other government decisions, the right to an institutional hearing to present the grievance and positions and arguments related to it, and to request redress of and relief from that grievance.

UNIT 16
LEGAL PROFESSIONALS IN THE UNITED STATES

The legal industry is thriving and now is a great time to embark on a legal career. The delivery of legal services is a complex process that requires a team of skilled professionals to provide quality and cost-effective service. As a result, the legal field holds hundreds of legal career options encompassing a diverse range of skills, experience and education. Here are several types of legal professionals, who can help people in different ways:

> **Judges**

Justices of the U.S. Supreme Court and circuit and district judges are **appointed** by the President of the United States if approved by a majority vote of the U.S. Senate. These justices and judges serve "**during good behavior**" —in effect, a life term. Presidents usually **nominate** persons to be judges who are members of their own political party. Persons appointed are usually distinguished lawyers, law professors, or lower federal court or state court judges. Once these judges are appointed their salaries cannot be reduced. Federal judges may only be removed from office through an impeachment process in which charges are made by the House of Representatives and a trial is conducted by the Senate. In the entire history of the United States, only a few judges have been **impeached** and those removed were found to have committed serious **misconduct**. These protections allow federal judges to exercise independent judgment without political or outside interference or influence.

The methods of selecting state judges vary from state to state and are often different within a state, depending on the type of court. The most common selection systems are **by commission nomination** and **by popular election**. In the commission nomination system, judges are appointed by the governor (the state's chief executive) who must choose from a list of candidates selected by an independent commission made up of lawyers, legislators, lay citizens, and sometimes judges. In many states judges are selected by popular election. These elections may be **partisan** or **non-partisan**. Candidates for judicial appointment or election must meet certain qualifications, such as being a **practicing** lawyer for a certain number of years. With very few exceptions, state judges serve specified, renewable terms. All states have procedures governing judicial conduct, discipline, and **removal**.

In both the federal and state systems, judicial candidates are almost always lawyers with many years of experience. There is no specific course of training for judges and no examination. Some states require judges to attend continuing education programs to learn about developments in the law. Both the federal and state court systems offer beginning and continuing education programs for judges.

➢ **Prosecutors**

Prosecutors in the federal system are part of the U.S. Department of Justice in the executive branch. **The Attorney General of the United States**, who heads the Department of Justice, is appointed by the President with Senate confirmation. The chief prosecutors in the federal court districts are called U.S. attorneys and are also appointed by the President with Senate confirmation. Within the Department of Justice is the Federal Bureau of Investigation, which investigates crimes against the United States.

Each **state** also has an **attorney general** in the state executive branch who is usually elected by the citizens of that state. There are also prosecutors in different regions of the state, **called state's attorneys** or **district attorneys**. These prosecutors are also usually elected.

➢ **Lawyers**

The legal system in the United States uses **the adversarial process**. Lawyers are essential to this process. Lawyers are responsible for presenting their clients' evidence and legal arguments to the court. Based on the lawyers' presentations, a trial judge or jury determines the facts and applies the law to reach a decision before judgment is entered.

Individuals are free to represent themselves in American courts, but lawyers are often necessary to present cases effectively. An individual who cannot afford to hire a lawyer may attempt to obtain one through a local legal aid society. Persons accused of crimes who cannot afford a lawyer are represented by a court-appointed attorney or by federal or state **public defender** offices.

American lawyers are licensed by the individual states in which they practice law. There is no national authority that licenses lawyers. Most states require applicants to hold a law degree (Juris Doctor) from an **accredited** law school. Also, most states require that applicants for a license to practice law pass a written bar examination and meet certain standards of character.

New Words & Expressions

justice	[ˈdʒʌstɪs]	n.	法官;司法;公正
appointed	[əˈpɔɪntɪd]	adj.	被任命的,指定的
during good behavior			品德良好期间，应规规矩矩
nominate	[ˈnɒmɪneɪt]	vt.	推荐,提名
impeach	[ɪmˈpiːtʃ]	vt.	弹劾;控告
misconduct	[ˌmɪsˈkɒndʌkt]	n.	不端行为,处理不当
by commission nomination			委员会提名
by popular election			全民选举
partisan	[ˌpɑːtɪˈzæn]	adj.	党派性的,偏袒的
		n.	党人,党徒;
non-partisan		adj.	无党派的
practicing	[ˈpræktɪsɪŋ]	adj.	（律师、医生等）执业的
removal	[rɪˈmuːvl]	n.	免职,移除
prosecutor	[ˈprɒsɪkjuːtə(r)]	n.	检察官

UNIT 16
LEGAL PROFESSIONALS IN THE UNITED STATES

the Attorney General of the United States			（美国）司法部长
state attorney general			州总检察长，州首席检察官
state's attorney / district attorney			州检察官（作为州政府代理人以州法起诉罪犯）
the adversarial process			（诉讼）对抗制
accredited	[əˈkredɪtɪd]	adj.	认可的，公认的
public defender			公设辩护人

Exercises

I. Choose the best answer to complete the following statements

1. Justices of the U.S. Supreme Court and circuit and district judges _____.

    A. appointed by the President of the United States

    B. are approved by a majority vote of the U.S. Senate

    C. are appointed by commission nomination and by popular election

    D. are appointed by the U. S. President with the approval of a majority vote of the U.S. Senate

2. Federal judges may only be removed from office _____.

    A. through an impeachment process

    B. by the President of the United States

    C. by the Attorney General of the United States

    D. through the trial conducted by the Senate

3. When selecting state judges, in the commission nomination system, judges are _____.

    A. elected by citizens of the state

    B. appointed by the district court

    C. appointed by the governor of the state(the state's chief executive)

D. elected by the justices in the Supreme Court

4. Prosecutors in the federal system are part of the U.S. Department of Justice in _____.

   A. the legislative branch

   B. the executive branch

   C. the judicial branch

   D. the U. S. Congress

5. The legal system of the United States uses the adversarial process according to which _____.

   A. individuals cannot represent themselves in court

   B. lawyers are essential to this process

   C. an individual who cannot afford to hire a lawyer must represent himself/herself in court

   D. a trial judge or jury are responsible for legal arguments to the court

II. Choose the proper words from the list below to fill in the blanks. Change the form of the words if necessary.

> appoint / general / approve / impeach / license
> nominate / practice, evidence / accredit / defend

Justices of the U.S. Supreme Court and circuit and district judges are ___1___ by U. S. President and ___2___ by a majority vote of the U.S. Senate. Federal judges may only be removed from office through a(n) ___3___ process in which charges are made by the House of Representatives and a trial is conducted by the Senate. The most common selection systems of state judges are by commission ___4___ and by popular election. Candidates for judicial appointment or election must meet certain qualifications, such as being a(n) ___5___ lawyer for a certain number of years. Each state also has an attorney ____6____ in the state executive branch who is usually elected by the citizens of that state. The legal system in the United States uses the adversarial process, in which lawyers are responsible for presenting their clients' ____7____ and legal arguments to the court. Persons accused of crimes who cannot afford a lawyer are represented by a court-appointed attorney or by federal or state public ____8____ offices. American lawyers are ____9____ by the individual states in which they practice law. Most states require applicants to hold a law degree (Juris Doctor) from a(n) ____10____ law school.

UNIT 17
LEGAL AID IN THE UNITED STATES

Legal aid in the United States appeared as early as the 1870s, but for the most part, the U.S. legal aid system remained **piecemeal** and **underfunded** until well into the 20th century. Defendants under criminal prosecution who cannot afford to hire an attorney are not only guaranteed **legal aid** related to the **charges**, but they are guaranteed legal representation in the form of public defenders as well.

History

In the early 1960s a new model for legal services emerged. Foundations, particularly the Ford Foundation, began to fund legal services programs located in multi-service social agencies, based on a philosophy that legal services should be a component of an overall anti-poverty effort.

In a series of cases, the U.S. Supreme Court ruled that American **indigents** do have a right to **counsel**, but only in criminal cases. See ***Gideon v. Wainwright***. A few states (like California) have also guaranteed the right to counsel for indigent defendants in "**quasi–criminal**" cases like **paternity actions** and involuntary terminations of parental rights. The federal government and some states have offices of **public defenders** who assist indigent defendants, while other states have systems for **outsourcing** the work to private lawyers.

In 1974, Congress created the Legal Services Corporation (LSC) to provide federal funding for civil (non-criminal) legal aid services. LSC's funding has **fluctuated** dramatically over the past three decades depending upon which political parties were in control of Congress and the White House. For example, LSC suffered **staggering** funding cuts under former President Ronald Reagan in the early 1980s (after he was unable to carry out his stated objective of abolishing LSC altogether). LSC funding flourished during the early years of President Bill Clinton's administration, but was severely cut again in 1995 after the Republican Party retook control of Congress.

System at Present

Legal aid for civil cases is currently provided by a variety of public interest law firms and community legal clinics, who often have "legal aid" or "legal services" in their names. Such firms may impose **income** and resource ceilings as well as restrictions on the types of cases they will take, because there are always too many potential clients and not enough money to go around. Common types of cases include: denial or **deprivation** of government benefits, **evictions**, **domestic violence**, immigration status, and **discrimination**. Some legal aid organizations serve as outside counsel to small nonprofit organizations that lack **in-house counsel**. Funding usually comes from charities, private donors, the federal government and some local and state governments. Most typical legal aid work involves counseling, informal negotiation, and appearances in **administrative** hearings, as opposed to formal litigation in the courts. However, the discovery of severe or recurring injustice with a large number of victims will sometimes justify the cost of large-scale impact litigation. Education and law reform activities are also sometimes undertaken.

Legal aid organizations that take LSC money tend to have more staff and services and can help more clients, but must also conform to strict government regulations that require careful timekeeping and prohibit **lobbying** and **class actions**. Many legal aid organizations refuse to take LSC money, and can continue to file class actions and directly lobby legislatures on behalf of the poor. Many organizations that provide civil legal services are heavily dependent on Interest on Lawyer Trust Accounts for funding.

However, even with supplemental funding from LSC, the total amount of legal aid available for civil cases is still grossly inadequate. According to LSC's widely released 2005 report "Documenting the Justice Gap in America: The Current Unmet Civil Legal Needs of Low-Income Americans," all legal aid offices nationwide, LSC-funded or not, are together able to meet only about 20 percent of the estimated legal needs of low-income people in the United States.

Pro Bono

The problem of chronic underfunding of legal aid traps the lower middle class in no-man's-land: too rich to qualify for legal aid, too poor to pay an attorney in private practice. To **remedy** the ongoing shortage of legal aid services, some commentators have suggested that **mandatory** pro bono obligations ought to be required of all lawyers, just as physicians working in emergency rooms are required to treat all patients regardless of ability to pay. However, most such proposals have been successfully fought off by bar associations. A notable exception is the Orange County Bar Association in Orlando, Florida, which requires all bar members to participate in its Legal Aid Society, by either serving in a pro bono capacity or donating a fee **in lieu of** service. Even where mandatory pro bono exists, however, funding for legal aid remains severely insufficient to provide assistance to a majority of those in need.

New Words & Expressions

piecemeal	[ˈpiːsmiːl]	adv.	零碎地；逐个地
		adj.	零碎的；逐渐的
underfunded	[ˌʌndəˈfʌndɪd]	adj.	资金不足的
legal aid			法律援助
charge	[tʃɑːdʒ]	n.	控告
		vt.	使承担，控告
indigent	[ˈɪndɪdʒənt]	adj.	贫困的；贫穷的
counsel	[ˈkaʊnsl]	n.	法律顾问；忠告
		vt.	建议；劝告
		vi.	商讨；提出忠告
quasi-criminal			准刑事的
paternity action			确认生父之诉

UNIT 17
LEGAL AID IN THE UNITED STATES

public defenders			公设辩护人
outsource	[ˈaʊtsɔːs]	vt.	把……外包
		vi.	外包
fluctuate	[ˈflʌktʃueɪt]	vi.	波动；涨落；动摇
		vt.	使波动；使动摇
staggering	[ˈstæɡərɪŋ]	adj.	惊人的，令人震惊的
impose	[ɪmˈpəʊz]	vt.	强加
deprivation	[ˌdeprɪˈveɪʃn]	n.	剥夺
eviction	[ɪˈvɪkʃn]	n.	逐出；赶出
domestic violence			家庭暴力
discrimination	[dɪˌskrɪmɪˈneɪʃn]	n.	歧视；区别
in-house counsel			公司内部法律顾问
administrative	[ədˈmɪnɪstrətɪv]	adj.	行政的
lobbying	[ˈlɒbɪ]	n.	游说
		v.	进行游说（lobby 的 ing 形式）；对议员进行游说以影响其投票
class action			集体诉讼
pro bono			无偿的；为了公益；为慈善机构和穷人提供的免费专业服务
remedy	[ˈremədɪ]	vt.	补救；治疗；纠正
		n.	补救；治疗；赔偿
mandatory	[ˈmændətərɪ]	adj.	强制的
in lieu of			代替

Exercises

I. Choose the best answer for each of the following questions.

1. What is legal aid?

A. Legal aid is a legal service provided for the public.

B. Legal aid refers to the process in which an expert in a certain area gives professional advice to the court.

C. Legal aid refers to a system in which the government pays for people to get advice about the law or to be represented in court when they do not have enough money for this.

D. Legal aid refers to a person's authority under law to engage in a particular undertaking or maintain a particular status.

2. What are public defenders?

A. Public defenders are the lawyers who represent a large group of people in class actions.

B. Public defenders are the lawyers who constitute a legal department within the corporation and represent that corporation.

C. Public defenders are the lawyers who represent states both in and out of court.

D. Public defenders are the lawyers who are paid by the government to represent defendants in the court if they cannot pay for themselves.

3. Which of the following statements about the Legal Services Corporation (LSC) is Not true?

A. LSC provides federal funding for legal aid organizations in civil cases.

B. LSC provides federal funding for the offices of public defenders in criminal cases.

C. LSC' funding depends on which political parties were in control of Congress and the White House.

D. LSC is created by the US Congress.

4. The legal aid in the civil cases does NOT involve _____.

A. formal litigation in the courts

B. counseling

C. informal negotiation

D. appearances in administrative hearings

UNIT 17
LEGAL AID IN THE UNITED STATES

5. Why do many legal aid organizations refuse to take LSC money?

   A. Because they have enough funding from charities, private donors.

   B. Because they can provide civil legal services dependent on Interest on Lawyer Trust Accounts for funding.

   C. Because they don't want to be restricted by government regulations.

   D. Because they don't want to be evaluated by LSC.

6. What does "mandatory pro bono obligations" mean?

   A. the requirement to work for the public good without compensation

   B. the improper performance of some act or duty

   C. the action or process of evicting a tenant from property

   D. prohibition on the transportation of goods into or out of a county

II. Match each legal term with its proper definition.

_____ 1. charge   a. to correct or improve a situation

_____ 2. deprivation   b. the lawyers who constitute a legal department within the corporation and represent that corporation

_____ 3. in-house counsel   c. a type of lawsuit that is started by a group of people who have the same problem

_____ 4. remedy   d. the fact of having representatives who will speak or vote for you or on your behalf

_____ 5. eviction   e. an official claim made by the police that sb has committed a crime

_____ 6. in lieu of   f. in place of

_____ 7. class action   g. the state of being without or denied something

_____ 8. discrimination   h. required by law

_____ 9. mandatory   i. the process of forcing someone to leave the house they are living in, usually because they have not paid their rent

_____ 10. representation j. the practice of treating sb. or a particular group in society less fairly than others

UNIT 18
LEGAL EDUCATION IN THE UNITED STATES

Becoming a lawyer in the United States requires a structured curriculum that is made up of high standards and academically rigorous classes. By better understanding legal education in the U.S., you will be better prepared to decide if a career in law is right for you. You can start your path to a career in law as soon as you complete your high school diploma. As an overview, here are the most important steps that will lead you to a successful career as an attorney:

1. Bachelor's degree at university or college — approximately 4 years
2. **LSAT** preparation exam — determined by your aptitude and law school
3. Law school to earn **Juris Doctor** — approximately 3 years
4. Bar examination — immediately after law school
5. Certification to practice law — received after passage of **bar exam**

Pre-Law

Legal education in the U.S. is unique since there is no formalized law program upon completing high school. Instead, students complete their undergraduate degree in their subject of choice. This provides students with the opportunity to study any subject before deciding that a career in law is right for them. To complete their undergraduate degree, American students go to a college or university to receive their bachelor's degree. A bachelor's degree in the U.S. is usually four years but can range from two to six years and certifies full-time studies within a particular subject. The subject that the student specializes in is also known as the student's major. Because there is no defined path to study law at this point in the education, it is important for students to concentrate on building their **oratory**, written, analytical, and critical thinking skills.

According to the American Bar Association (ABA), a volunteer organization of lawyers and law students that sets standards for the American legal profession, "the ABA does not recommend any undergraduate majors or group of courses to prepare for a legal education. Students are admitted to law school from almost every **academic discipline**." So there is truly no required course at all to get into law school — great lawyers can start as English majors, history majors, engineers, doctors, pilots, builders and everything in between.

Most law schools evaluate a student's academic performance based on their grade point average (GPA). A grade point average measures a student's academic achievement over the course of their degree usually out of a scale of 4.0. This number is a critical indicator for law schools as, together with the LSAT score, it is used to predict future performance in law school. Students are therefore encouraged to study a field of interest where they will both earn high grades and that will also improve writing, speaking, critical thinking and problem solving skills.

LSAT Exam

Another important factor in law school admissions is the Law School Admission Test (LSAT). For many, this is the first step toward a career in law. Many students will take the LSAT exam if they plan to continue to law school immediately after graduating with their Bachelor's degree. Other students may join the work force before they determine that a career in law is right for them. In either case, the true first step to becoming an attorney is sitting for the LSAT exam. Law schools use the LSAT as an important indicator of a student's potential for success in law school.

The LSAT exam is a standardized test administered four times a year testing student's analytical and logical reasoning skills. Lasting half a day, students complete five sections of multiple choice questions along with a written section that is sent directly to law schools unscored. Many students spend months prior to the exam taking sample tests and using external resources like tutors and prep classes to prepare themselves. It is important for students to do well since all results, even if students retake the exam, will be sent to admissions for review. Additionally, under normal circumstances, individuals cannot take the LSAT more than three times in any two-year period so it is important to come to the testing center prepared.

Law School

Applying to law school in the U.S. is not an easy process. Law school selection alone can be difficult. The ABA recognizes over 200 **accredited** institutions in the US including private law schools, public law schools, law schools **affiliated** with larger colleges/universities, and even independent law schools. Once your application has been evaluated, you may just be lucky enough to receive a welcome letter in the mail. If you are accepted to law school, it's time for you to mentally prepare. Many students say that law school is a difficult challenge, especially in the first year where you are adjusting to a new, academically challenging schedule and environment.

Students are typically referred to as 1Ls in their first year of law school, 2Ls in their second year of law school, and finally 3Ls in their third year of law school. Students can expect to take courses covering **constitutional law**, **civil procedure**, contracts, evidence, criminal law, **torts**, legal writing and research, and **property law** just to name a few courses. Most 1Ls have a set curriculum that is developed by the school to provide students the exposure they need. At the same time, the first year also serves to lay the foundation of skills as students continue their legal education in the U.S. 2Ls and 3Ls are usually able to choose their own classes based on their interest of legal study such as family law, tax law, international law, etc.

Schools generally vary in curriculum so it is important to investigate classes, teaching methods, evaluation, and more, even before you submit your application. Many law classes focus on analyzing legal issues, reading cases, identifying the facts, and finally applying law to these facts. Finally, once you successfully complete your 3-year law school, you will be issued your Juris Doctor degree (J.D.) which will allow you to sit for the bar examination.

Bar Examination

The bar examination in the United States is required before students begin practicing law. In order to receive a license, students must contact the state board of bar examiners to schedule a time to sit for the test. These licenses provide **authorization** to practice in that state alone. Students who intend to practice in multiple U.S. states investigate which other U.S. states will allow them to "waive" into their state bar — no one wants to sit for multiple state bar exams if it can be avoided. Once students have determined the state in which they'd like to practice, the next step is to register for the state administered bar exam. Most bar exams are approximately two days long and a few states have three day exams. There are multiple choice and essay questions designed to test knowledge on general legal principles across a wide variety of topics, and knowledge of state-specific laws and principles.

New Words & Expressions

LSAT: Law School Admission Test			法学院入学考试
Juris Doctor: or J.D.			法学博士
bar examination			律师资格考试
certify	[ˈsəːtɪfaɪ]		证明；保证
oratory	[ˈɒrətrɪ]	n.	讲演术；演说
academic discipline			学科
accredited		adj.	被认可的；可接受的；委任的
affiliate	[əˈfɪlɪeɪt]	vt.	使隶属于；接纳；追溯
		vi.	发生联系
constitutional law			宪法
civil procedure			民事诉讼法
torts			侵权法
property law			物权法
authorization	[ˌɔːθəraɪˈzeɪʃn]	n.	授权(书)；批准

UNIT 18
LEGAL EDUCATION IN THE UNITED STATES

Exercises

I. Choose the best answer for each of the following questions.

1. What makes legal education in America unique?

    A. Law students in America have to take bar examination before being qualified as an attorney.

    B. American students can apply for law school upon high school graduation.

    C. There's no undergraduate degree in law.

    D. American students have to take a standardized admission test before going to a law school.

2. Which two factors are important in law school admission?

    A. Grade point average (GPA) and the Law School Admission Test (LSAT)

    B. a student's major and grade point average (GPA)

    C. a student's major and the Law School Admission Test (LSAT)

    D. the Law School Admission Test (LSAT) and a student's working experience.

3. Which of the following statements is NOT true about LSAT?

    A. LSAT is used to evaluate a student's potential for future success in law school.

    B. LSAT tests students' analytical and logical reasoning skills.

    C. LSAT is held four times a year and an applicant cannot take the test more than four times in any two-year period.

    D. ALL of an applicant's LSAT scores will be sent for consideration in admission if he/she take the exam for multiple times.

4. What kind of organization is the American Bar Association (ABA)?

    A. a governmental organization of lawyers and law students

    B. a governmental organization that sets standards for the American legal profession

    C. a volunteer organization of lawyers

    D. a volunteer organization of lawyers and law students that sets standards for the

American legal profession

5. In which year of law school, students receive a set of mandatory courses and develop fundamental skills?

   A. the first year

   B. the second year

   C. the third year

   D. all the three years

6. Which of the following statements is true?

   A. J.D degree is not necessary to sit for the bar examination.

   B. The license issued by one state administered bar examination allows one to practice law in that state alone.

   C. The license issued by one state administered bar examination allows one to practice law in multiple states.

   D. All the bar exams last for approximately two days.

II. Choose the proper words from the list below to fill in the blanks. Change the form of the words if necessary.

> branch / reflect / professional / acquisition / legal
> encounter / particular / analytical / graduate / share / fundamentally

Students thinking of law study soon discover that the programs of most law schools have a great deal in common. The similarity is natural, since most American law schools ____1____ the aim of educating lawyers for careers that may take many paths and that will frequently not be limited to any ____2____ state or region. Although many lawyers eventually find themselves practicing within some special ____3____ of the law, American legal education is still ____4____ an education for generalists. It emphasizes the ____5____ of broad and basic knowledge of law,

UNIT 18
LEGAL EDUCATION IN THE UNITED STATES

understanding of the functioning of the ____6____ system, and development of ____7____ abilities of a high order. This common emphasis ____8____ the conviction that such an education is the best kind of preparation for the diverse roles that law school ____9____ occupy in American life and for the changing nature of the problems any individual lawyer is likely to ____10____ over a long career. Within this tradition some schools combine an emphasis on technical legal knowledge and ____11____ skills with a concern for illuminating the connections between law and the social forces with which it interacts.

UNIT 19
WORLD TRADE ORGANIZATION (I)

The World Trade Organization (WTO), headquartered in Geneva, Switzerland, is an intergovernmental organization which regulates international trade. The WTO officially **commenced** on 1 January 1995 under the Marrakesh Agreement, signed by 123 nations on 15 April 1994, replacing the General Agreement on Tariffs and Trade (GATT), which commenced in 1948. The WTO deals with regulation of trade between participating countries by providing a **framework** for negotiating trade agreements and a dispute resolution process aimed at enforcing participants' **adherence** to WTO agreements, which are signed by representatives of member governments and **ratified** by their parliaments.

The WTO is attempting to complete negotiations on the Doha Development Round, which was launched in 2001 with an **explicit** focus on developing countries. As of June 2012, the future of **the Doha Round** remained uncertain. The conflict between free trade on industrial goods and services but **retention** of **protectionism** on **farm subsidies** to domestic agricultural sector (requested by developed countries) and the **substantiation** of fair trade on agricultural products (requested by developing countries) remain the major obstacles. This **impasse** has made it impossible to launch new WTO negotiations beyond the Doha Development Round.

History

The WTO's predecessor, **the General Agreement on Tariffs and Trade** (GATT), was established after World War II in the wake of other new multilateral institutions dedicated to international economic cooperation — notably the **Bretton Woods institutions** known as the World Bank and the International Monetary Fund.

UNIT 19
WORLD TRADE ORGANIZATION (I)

The GATT was the only **multilateral** instrument governing international trade from 1946 until the WTO was established on 1 January 1995. Seven rounds of negotiations occurred under GATT. The first real GATT trade rounds concentrated on further reducing **tariffs**. Then, the Kennedy Round in the mid-sixties brought about a GATT **anti-dumping** Agreement and a section on development. The Tokyo Round during the seventies was the first major attempt to tackle trade barriers that do not take the form of tariffs, and to improve the system, adopting a series of agreements on non-tariff barriers, which in some cases interpreted existing GATT rules, and in others broke entirely new ground.

Well before GATT's 40th anniversary, its members concluded that the GATT system was straining to adapt to a new globalizing world economy. In response to the problems identified, the eighth GATT round — known as **the Uruguay Round** — was launched in September 1986, in Uruguay. It was the biggest negotiating mandate on trade ever agreed: the talks were going to extend the trading system into several new areas, notably trade in services and **intellectual property**, and to reform trade in the sensitive sectors of agriculture and **textiles**; all the original GATT articles were up for review. The Final Act concluding the Uruguay Round and officially establishing the WTO regime was signed 15 April 1994, during the ministerial meeting at Marrakesh, Morocco, and hence is known as the Marrakesh Agreement.

The GATT still exists as the WTO's **umbrella treaty** for trade in goods, updated as a result of the Uruguay Round negotiations. GATT 1994 is not however the only legally **binding** agreement included via the Final Act at Marrakesh; a long list of about 60 agreements, **annexes**, decisions and understandings was adopted. The agreements fall into a structure with six main parts:

➤ The Agreement Establishing the WTO
➤ Goods and investment — the Multilateral Agreements on Trade in Goods including the GATT 1994 and the Trade Related Investment Measures (TRIMS)
➤ Services — the General Agreement on Trade in Services (GATS)

> Intellectual property — the Agreement on Trade-Related Aspects of Intellectual Property Rights (TRIPS)
> Dispute settlement Understanding (DSU)
> Reviews of governments' trade policies (TPRM)

Organizational Structure

Ministerial conference: The highest decision-making body of the WTO is the Ministerial Conference, which usually meets every two years. It brings together all members of the WTO, all of which are countries or customs unions. The Ministerial Conference can take decisions on all matters under any of the multilateral trade agreements.

The General Council: It is the WTO's highest-level decision-making body in Geneva, meeting regularly to carry out the functions of the WTO. It has representatives (usually ambassadors or equivalent) from all member governments and has the authority to act on behalf of the ministerial conference which only meets about every two years. The General Council has the following subsidiary bodies which oversee committees in different areas: Council for Trade in Goods, Council for Trade-Related Aspects of Intellectual Property Rights, and Council for Trade in Services, Trade Negotiations Committee.

Membership and Accession

The WTO currently has 162 members, of which 117 are developing countries or separate customs territories. The process of becoming a WTO member is unique to each applicant country, and the terms of **accession** are dependent upon the country's stage of economic development and current trade regime.

A country wishing to accede to the WTO submits an application to the General Council, and has to describe all aspects of its trade and economic policies that **have a bearing on** WTO agreements. The working party determines the terms and conditions of entry into the WTO for the applicant nation, and may consider transitional periods to allow countries some **leeway** in complying with the WTO rules. The final phase of accession involves bilateral negotiations between the applicant nation and other working party members regarding the **concessions** and **commitments** on tariff levels and market access for goods and services. When the bilateral talks conclude, the working party sends to the general council or ministerial conference an accession package, which includes a summary of all the working party meetings, the **Protocol of Accession** (a draft membership treaty), and lists ("schedules") of the member-to-be's commitments. Once the general council or ministerial conference approves of the terms of accession, the applicant's parliament must ratify the Protocol of Accession before it can become a member.

Decision-Making

The WTO describes itself as a rules-based, member-driven organization — all decisions are made by the member governments, and the rules are the outcome of negotiations among members. The WTO Agreement foresees votes where **consensus** cannot be reached, but the practice of consensus dominates the process of decision-making.

New Words & Expressions

commence	[kəˈmens]	v.	开始；着手
framework	[ˈfreɪmwɜːk]	n.	框架；机制；准则
adherence	[ədˈhɪərəns]	n.	遵守，坚持
ratify	[ˈrætɪfaɪ]	vt.	批准
explicit	[ɪkˈsplɪsɪt]	adj.	明确的；清楚的；直率的；详述的
the Doha Round			多哈回合
retention	[rɪˈtenʃn]	n.	保留；扣留，滞留
protectionism	[prəˈtekʃənɪzəm]	n.	保护主义，贸易保护主义；贸易保护制度
farm subsidy			农业补贴
substantiation	[səbˌstænʃɪˈeɪʃn]	n.	证实；实体化

impasse	[ˈæmpɑːs]	n.	僵局；死路
the General Agreement on Tariffs and Trade			关贸总协定
Bretton Woods institutions			布雷顿森林机构
multilateral	[ˌmʌltɪˈlætərəl]	adj.	多边的；多国的，多国参加的
tariff	[ˈtærɪf]	n.	关税
the anti-dumping Agreement			反倾销协议
the Uruguay Round			乌拉圭回合
intellectual property			知识产权
textile	[ˈtekstaɪl]	n.	纺织品，织物
		adj.	纺织的
umbrella treaty			总括条约
binding	[ˈbaɪndɪŋ]	adj.	有约束力的；捆绑的
annex	[əˈneks]	vt.	附加；获得；并吞
		n.	附加物；附属建筑物
ministerial	[ˌmɪnɪˈstɪərɪəl]	adj.	部长的；内阁的
The General Council			常务理事会
accession	[ækˈseʃn]	n.	增加；就职；到达
have a bearing on			与……有关系
leeway	[ˈliːweɪ]	n.	余地
concession	[kənˈseʃn]	n.	让步；特许（权）；承认；退位
commitment	[kəˈmɪtmənt]	n.	承诺，保证；委托；承担义务；献身
the Protocol of Accession			加入议定书
consensus	[kənˈsensəs]	n.	一致

Exercises

I. Choose the best answer for each of the following questions.

1. Which of the following organizations is the predecessor of WTO?

UNIT 19
WORLD TRADE ORGANIZATION (I)

   A. the International Monetary Fund

   B. the General Agreement on Tariffs and Trade

   C. the International Trade Organization

   D. the World Bank

2. WTO is an intergovernmental organization governing _____.

   A. government policies of the world

   B. the international athletic events

   C. the international currencies

   D. the international trade

3. Which GATT round of negotiations leads to the birth of WTO?

   A. the Kennedy Round

   B. the Uruguay Round

   C. the Tokyo Round

   D. the Doha Round

4. What is the main issue in the Doha Round?

   A. the conflict between developing countries and developed countries on the fair trade of the agricultural products

   B. the conflict between developing countries and developed countries on the tariff ceiling

   C. the conflict between developing countries and developed countries on free trade of industrial goods.

   D. the conflict between developing countries and developed countries on free trade of services

5. Which of the following statements about the WTO agreements is NOT true?

   A. The WTO agreements are signed by representatives of its member governments and ratified by their parliaments.

   B. The GATT still exists as the WTO's umbrella treaty and GATT 1994 is the only legally binding agreement on WTO member countries.

C. The WTO agreements fall into a structure with six main parts.

D. The trades among the WTO members are regulated by the WTO agreements.

6. Ministerial conference is the highest decision-making body of the WTO which meets _____.

   A. regularly   B. every year   C. every two years   D. every three years

7. In order to become a WTO member, a country need _____.

   A. submit an application to the General Council, which describe all aspects of its trade and economic policies that have a bearing on WTO agreements

   B. have bilateral negotiations with other working party members regarding the concessions and commitments on tariff levels and market access for goods and services

   C. ratify the Protocol of Accession by its parliament

   D. all of the above

II. Write the full name of the following abbreviations and then translate them into Chinese.

1. WTO (　　　　　　)　_____
2. GATT (　　　　　　)　_____
3. GATS (　　　　　　)　_____
4. TRIPS (　　　　　　)　_____
5. TRIMS (　　　　　　)　_____

III. Translate the following paragraph into Chinese.

The World Trade Organization (WTO), headquartered in Geneva, Switzerland, is an intergovernmental organization which regulates international trade. The WTO officially commenced on 1 January 1995 under the Marrakesh Agreement, signed by 123 nations on 15 April 1994, replacing the General Agreement on Tariffs and

UNIT 19
WORLD TRADE ORGANIZATION (I)

Trade (GATT), which commenced in 1948. The WTO deals with regulation of trade between participating countries by providing a framework for negotiating trade agreements and a dispute resolution process aimed at enforcing participants' adherence to WTO agreements, which are signed by representatives of member governments and ratified by their parliaments.

UNIT 20

WORLD TRADE ORGANIZATION (II)

Among the various functions of the WTO, these are regarded by analysts as the most important:

➢ It **oversees** the **implementation**, administration and operation of **the covered agreements**.

➢ It provides a **forum** for negotiations and for settling disputes.

Additionally, it is the WTO's duty to review and **propagate** the national trade policies, and to ensure the **coherence** and **transparency** of trade policies through **surveillance** in global economic policy-making. Another **priority** of the WTO is the assistance of developing, least-developed and low-income countries in **transition** to adjust to WTO rules and disciplines through technical cooperation and training.

As globalization proceeds in today's society, the necessity of an International Organization to manage the trading systems has been of vital importance. As the **trade volume** increases, issues such as protectionism, trade barriers, subsidies, **violation** of intellectual property arise due to the differences in the trading rules of every nation. The World Trade Organization serves as the **mediator** between the nations when such problems arise. WTO could be referred to as the product of globalization and also as one of the most important organizations in today's globalized society.

The WTO is also a center of economic research and analysis: regular **assessments** of the global trade picture in its annual publications and research reports on specific topics are produced by the organization.

Finally, With a view to achieving greater coherence in global economic policy making, the WTO shall cooperate with the international Monetary Fund (IMF) and with the International Bank for Reconstruction and Development (IBRD) and its **affiliated** agencies.

Dispute Settlement

The WTO's dispute-settlement system is the result of the evolution of rules, procedures and practices developed over almost half a century under the GATT 1947. In 1994, the WTO members agreed on the Understanding on Rules and Procedures Governing the Settlement of Disputes (DSU) annexed to the "Final Act" signed in Marrakesh in 1994. Dispute settlement is regarded by the WTO as the central **pillar** of the multilateral trading system, and as a unique contribution to the stability of the global economy. WTO members have agreed that, if they believe fellow-members are violating trade rules, they will use the multilateral system of settling disputes instead of taking action **unilaterally**.

The operation of the WTO dispute settlement process involves case-specific panels appointed by the Dispute Settlement Body (DSB), the Appellate Body, The **Director–General** and the WTO Secretariat, **arbitrators**, and advisory experts.

The priority is to settle disputes, preferably through a mutually agreed solution, and provision has been made for the process to be conducted in an efficient and timely manner so that if a case is **adjudicated**, it should normally take no more than one year for a panel ruling and no more than 16 months if the case is appealed; if the complainant deems the case urgent, consideration of the case should take even less time. WTO member nations are obliged to accept the process as **exclusive** and compulsory.

Principles of the Trading System

The WTO establishes a framework for trade policies; it does not define or specify outcomes. That is, it is concerned with setting the rules of the trade policy games. Five principles are of particular importance in understanding both the pre-1994 GATT and the WTO:

1. Non-discrimination. It has two major components: **the most favored nation (MFN) rule**, and **the national treatment policy**. Both are embedded in the main

WTO rules on goods, services, and intellectual property, but their precise scope and nature differ across these areas. The MFN rule requires that a WTO member must apply the same conditions on all trade with other WTO members, i.e, a WTO member has to grant the most favorable conditions under which it allows trade in a certain product type to all other WTO members. "Grant someone a special favor and you have to do the same for all other WTO members." National treatment means that imported goods should be treated no less favorably than domestically produced goods (at least after the foreign goods have entered the market) and was introduced to tackle non-tariff barriers to trade (e.g. technical standards, security standards et al. discriminating against imported goods).

2. **Reciprocity**. It reflects both a desire to limit the scope of free-riding that may arise because of the MFN rule, and a desire to obtain better access to foreign markets. A related point is that for a nation to negotiate, it is necessary that the gain from doing so be greater than the gain available from unilateral liberalization; reciprocal concessions intend to ensure that such gains will materialize.

3. Binding and enforceable commitments. The tariff commitments made by WTO members in a multilateral trade negotiation and on accession are **enumerated** in a schedule (list) of concessions. These schedules establish "ceiling bindings": a country can change its bindings, but only after negotiating with its trading partners, which could mean compensating them for loss of trade. If satisfaction is not obtained, the complaining country may **invoke** the WTO dispute settlement procedures.

4. Transparency. The WTO members are required to publish their trade regulations, to maintain institutions allowing for the review of administrative decisions affecting trade, to respond to requests for information by other members, and to notify changes in trade policies to the WTO. These internal transparency requirements are supplemented and **facilitated** by periodic country-specific reports (trade policy reviews) through **the Trade Policy Review Mechanism (TPRM)**. The WTO system tries also to improve predictability and stability, discouraging the use of **quotas** and other measures used to set limits on quantities of imports.

UNIT 20
WORLD TRADE ORGANIZATION (II)

5. Safety valves. In specific circumstances, governments are able to restrict trade. The WTO's agreements permit members to take measures to protect not only the environment but also public health, animal health and plant health.

Exceptions to the MFN principle also allow for **preferential treatment** of developing countries, regional free trade areas and **customs unions**.

New Words & Expressions

oversee	[ˌəʊvəˈsiː]	vt.	监督；审查
implementation	[ˌɪmplɪmenˈteɪʃn]	n.	实现；履行
the covered agreements			适用协议
forum	[ˈfɔːrəm]	n.	论坛
propagate	[ˈprɒpəgeɪt]	vt.	传播；宣传
coherence	[kəʊˈhɪərəns]	n.	一致；连贯性；凝聚
transparency	[trænsˈpærənsi]	n.	透明，透明度
surveillance	[sɜːˈveɪləns]	n.	监督；监视
priority	[praɪˈɒrəti]	n.	优先；优先权
transition	[trænˈzɪʃn]	n.	过渡；转变
trade volume	[treɪd][ˈvɒljuːm]	n.	贸易额
violation	[ˌvaɪəˈleɪʃn]	n.	违反；妨碍，侵害；违背
mediator	[ˈmiːdieɪtə(r)]	n.	调解者
assessment	[əˈsesmənt]	n.	评定；估价
affiliate	[əˈfɪlieɪt]	vt.	使附属；接纳；使紧密联系
		vi.	参加，加入；发生联系
pillar	[ˈpɪlə(r)]	n.	柱子，柱形物；栋梁；墩
unilaterally	[ˌjuːnɪˈlætərəli]	adv.	单方面地
Director-General	[dɪˈrektə ˈdʒenərəl]	n.	总干事；理事长；署长
arbitrator	[ˈɑːbɪtreɪtə(r)]	n.	公断人，仲裁人

adjudicate	[əˈdʒuːdɪkeɪt]	vi.	裁定；宣判
		vt.	裁定；宣判
exclusive	[ɪkˈskluːsɪv]	adj.	独有的；排外的；专一的
the most favoured nation (MFN) rule			最惠国待遇
the national treatment policy			国民待遇
reciprocity	[ˌresɪˈprɒsəti]	n.	相互作用；相互性；互惠主义
enumerate	[ɪˈnjuːməreɪt]	vt.	列举；枚举；计算
invoke	[ɪnˈvəʊk]	vt.	调用；援引；引起；恳求
facilitate	[fəˈsɪlɪteɪt]	vt.	促进；帮助；使容易
the Trade Policy Review Mechanism (TPRM)			贸易政策审议机制
quota	[ˈkwəʊtə]	n.	配额；定额；限额
preferential treatment			特惠待遇
customs union			关税联盟

Exercises

I. Choose the proper words from the list below to fill in the blanks. Change the form of the words if necessary.

> implement / dispute / priority / violate / invoke
> complainant / compulsory / adjudicate / binding / mediate

1. We hope that this _____ can be settled through friendly negotiation without its being submitted for arbitration.

2. The arbitration shall take place in fifteen days. The decision of the Arbitration Commission shall be final and _____ on both parties.

3. The government's refusal to see that the protection of the environment must be our first _____ today is a great tragedy.

UNIT 20
WORLD TRADE ORGANIZATION (II)

4. The _____ and the respondent shall bear the burden of proofs for their own claims.

5. Tactics should be simple, easy to _____, and easy for customers to understand and follow.

6. United Nations officials have _____ a series of peace meetings between the two sides.

7. "China's handling does not _____ international rules and is not contrary to its WTO accession promises," the paper said.

8. It shall be prohibited to produce, sell or import products that are not up to the _____ standards.

9. Where the contract does not require the matter, it should _____ the provisions of the practice.

10. The international court of justice might be a suitable place to _____ claims.

II. Check (√) the functions of WTO.

_____ 1. to maintain peace and security for all of its member states

_____ 2. to protect human rights and provide humanitarian assistance when needed

_____ 3. to facilitate the implementation, administration and operation of WTO agreements

_____ 4. to review the national trade policies

_____ 5. to annually publishes the Human Development Index to rank countries in terms of poverty, literacy, education, and life expectancy

_____ 6. to provide a forum for negotiation and for setting disputes arising from the trades among member states.

_____ 7. to assist the developing countries in transition to adjust WTO rules through technical cooperation and training

III. Judge whether the statements below are true (T) or false (F).

_____ 1. The Trade Policy Review Mechanism (TPRM) is regarded as the central pillar of the multilateral trading system, which helps to stabilize the global economy.

_____ 2. If fellow-members violate trade rules, the other WTO members will have a joint economic sanction on those countries.

_____ 3. Normally it takes less than one year for a dispute-settling panel to rule a case and less than 16 months if the case is appealed.

_____ 4. The national treatment policy means that imported goods should be treated no less favorably than domestically produced goods.

_____ 5. The most favored nation (MFN) rule requires that a WTO member must apply favorable conditions on all trade with least-developed countries.

_____ 6. Under no circumstances can a member country change its tariff ceiling listed on accession.

_____ 7. In specific circumstances, governments are able to restrict trade due to the protection of the environment, public health, animal health and plant health.

_____ 8. The reciprocity principle reflects both a desire to limit the scope of free-riding that may arise because of the MFN rule, and a desire to obtain better access to foreign markets.

UNIT 21
CONSTITUTIONAL LAW

The Constitution is the supreme law of the United States of America. Constitutional law defines the relations between the president and congress and between the federal government and the states, and it regulates the government's ability to control abortion, to assess taxes, to build high-ways, to **designate** drug-free school zones, and to print stamps.

History

The United States Constitution was written in 1787 during the Philadelphia Convention. The old Congress set the rules the new government followed in terms of writing and **ratifying** the new constitution. After ratification in eleven states, in 1789 its elected officers of government **assembled** in New York City, replacing the Articles of Confederation government. The original Constitution has been **amended** twenty-seven times. The meaning of the Constitution is interpreted and extended by judicial review in the federal courts. The original **parchment** copies are on display at the National Archives Building.

Structure

The Constitution, originally comprising seven articles, **delineates** the national frame of government. Its first three articles **entrench** the **doctrine** of the separation of powers, whereby the federal government is divided into three branches: the legislative, consisting of the bicameral Congress; the executive, consisting of the President; and the judicial, consisting of the Supreme Court and other federal courts. Articles Four, Five and Six entrench concepts of federalism, describing the rights and responsibilities of state governments and of the states in relationship to the federal government. Article Seven establishes the procedure subsequently used by the thirteen States to ratify it.

Since the Constitution came into force in 1789, it has been amended twenty-seven times. In general, the first ten amendments, known collectively as the Bill of Rights, offer specific protections of individual liberty and justice and place restrictions on the powers of government. The majority of the seventeen later amendments expand individual civil rights protections. Others address issues related to federal authority or **modify** government processes and procedures. Amendments to the United States Constitution, unlike ones made to many constitutions world-wide, are appended to the end of the document. At seven articles and twenty-seven amendments, it is the shortest written constitution in force. All five pages of the original U.S. Constitution are written on parchment.

The Constitution is interpreted, supplemented, and implemented by a large body of constitutional law. The Constitution of the United States is the first constitution of its kind, adopted by the people's representatives for an expansive nation; and it has influenced the constitutions of other nations.

The Basic Principles of the United States Constitution

With a little more than 7,000 words, the Constitution can be easily read within half an hour. However, it lays out the basic principles on which the United States government operates on:

1. Limited Government

Limited government is a government outline where any more than minimal governmental intervention in personal liberties and the economy is not allowed by law, usually in a written Constitution. The U.S. Constitution is supposed to limit the power of the federal government in several ways: First, it prohibits the government from interfering with certain key areas, such as conscience, expression and association; Secondly, certain forms are established for the dealing of governments with their own citizens: specific actions are forbidden to the government; It was assumed that the Bill of Rights would be largely **self-enforcing**, and this solution proved to be inadequate to do more than slow the growth of government; Government powers were expanded, even while following the letter of the Bill of Rights, and increasingly, key elements were virtually ignored.

2. Separation of Powers

In a presidential government like the United States, all power is distributed among three branches: legislative, judicial, and executive. This is called the separation of powers. The Constitution talks about the separation of powers among the President, Congress, and the Supreme Court. Articles I, II, and III declare the separation of powers among those three branches. The separation of powers was designed not to take away power from the government, but to spread it out evenly among all parts of it.

3. Judicial Review

The power of judicial review is the power of the courts to determine whether or not the government has violated the laws of the Constitution. In other words, judicial review is the power to declare something unconstitutional, or against the constitution. The Supreme Court has used the power of judicial review in many cases throughout the nation. However, in most cases the Supreme Court found that the government was in fact being constitutional and not the other way around.

4. Due Process

Due process is the legal requirement that the state must respect all legal rights that are owed to a person. Due process balances the power of law of the land and protects the individual person from it. When a government harms a person without following the exact course of the law, this constitutes a due process violation, which offends the rule of law.

The Fifth and Fourteenth Amendments to the United States Constitution each contain a Due Process Clause. Due process deals with the administration of justice and thus the Due Process Clause acts as a safeguard from arbitrary denial of life, liberty, or property by the Government outside the sanction of law. The Supreme Court of the United States interprets the Clauses as providing four protections: procedural due process (in civil and criminal proceedings), substantive due process, a prohibition against vague laws, and as the vehicle for the incorporation of the Bill of Rights.

5. Checks and Balances

The United States government is broken into three branches: legislative, executive, and judicial. These branches are not completely separated or completely independent. There remains one relationship among the three — the system of checks and balances. This means that each branch is subject to the checks of the other two branches.

For example, Congress has the power to make a law, but the President can **veto** it, or reject it. And in the case of a veto, Congress may override that veto with a 2/3 vote. Take another example, the President has the power to appoint federal judges, but the **Senate** must approve that appointment with a majority vote. The system of checks and balances ties all three branches together.

New Words & Expressions

designate	['dezɪgneɪt]	vt.	指明，指出；指派；表明，意味着；把……定名为
		adj.	指定而尚未上任的；选出而尚未上任的
ratify	['rætɪfaɪ]	v.	批准；认可
assemble	[ə'sembl]	vt.& vi.	集合，收集
		vt.	装配，组合
amend	[ə'mend]	vt.& vi.	改良，修改；修订
parchment	['pɑːtʃmənt]	n.	羊皮纸；文凭；上等纸；羊皮纸古文稿
delineate	[dɪ'lɪnɪeɪt]	vt.	勾画，描述
entrench	[ɪn'trentʃ]	v.	用壕沟围绕或保护……；牢固地确立……；挖掘壕沟
		n.	壕沟；防御设施
doctrine	['dɒktrɪn]	n.	教条，教义；法律原则；声明；（古语）所教的东西，教育
modify	['mɒdɪfaɪ]	vi.	被修饰；修改
		vt.	改变；减轻，减缓；[语]修饰，（用变音符号）改变

self-enforcing		adj.	自我强制的,本身具有强制力的
veto	[ˈviːtəʊ]	n.	否决权,否认权；行使否决权；否决理由
		vt.	否决,不同意；不批准,禁止
		vi.	否决；禁止
Senate	[ˈsɛnɪt]	n.	参议院（美国、法国、澳大利亚等国家的两个立法机构之一）；上院；（某些国家的）大学理事会；大学评议会

Exercises

Ⅰ. Choose the best answer for each of the following questions.

1. The U.S. Constitution has as its most significant purposes_____.

    A. cconferring power on national and state government

    B. conferring power on the national government and limiting the power of national and state government

    C. limiting the power of national and state government

    D. conferring power on national government and limiting the power of national and state governments and private individuals

2. The Constitution was completed and signed by its writers on _____.

    A. July 4, 1776

    B. September 17, 1787

    C. May 30, 1863

    D. October 12, 1492

3. The first 10 amendments to the Constitution are called the _____.

    A. the Preamble

    B. the Bill of Rights

    C. the Articles

    D. separation of powers

4. The three parts of the Constitution are _____.

    A. legislative, executive, and judicial

    B. the Capitol, the White House, and the Library of Congress

    C. Article I, Article II, and Article III

    D. the preamble, the 7 articles, and the 27 amendments

5. Separation of powers _____.

    A. was something that the writers of the Constitution wanted to do

    B. was accomplished by dividing the national government into 3 branches

    C. meant that no one branch of government could become all powerful

    D. all of the above

II. Matching each legal term with proper definition

1. jurisprudence
2. federalism
3. invalidate
4. separation of powers
5. checks and balances
6. judicial review
7. judiciary
8. veto
9. removal
10. ratification

a. To make something illegal

b. A legal system

c. Division of governmental powers into three branches of government—legislative, executive, and judicial

d. Vote against

e. A court's power to review actions of other branches or levels of government

f. The branch of government responsible for interpreting the laws and administering justice

g. A power of one government branch to prohibit an action by another branch

h. The transfer or moving of a person or thing from one position, location to another

i. Adoption or enactment, esp. where the act is the last in a series of necessary steps or consents

j. the relationship between the individual states and the national government

UNIT 22
CONTRACTS

A contract is a legally **enforceable** agreement between two or more parties that creates an obligation to do or not do particular things. It's at the center of international business. In the United States, contracts are usually governed by the law in the state where the agreement was made. One of the most important statutes is the **Uniform Commercial Code** which is a very large collection of legal rules regarding many important business, or commercial activities.

Definition

The common law countries stress the contract as a kind of "promise", the civil law countries emphasize the "agreement between the parties." According to Restatement of the Law of Contracts: "A contract is a promise or a set of promise for the **breach** of which the law gives a remedy, or the performance of which the law in some way recognizes as a duty." The basic elements of a contract are mutual **assent**, **consideration**, capacity and legality. In some states, the element of consideration can be satisfied by a valid **substitute**. Possible remedies for breach of contract include general damages, **consequential** damages, **reliance** damages, and specific performance.

Commercial Use

Contracts are widely used in commercial law, and form the legal foundation for transactions across the world. Common examples include contracts for the sale of services and goods (both wholesale and retail), construction contracts, contracts of carriage, software licenses, employment contracts, insurance policies, sale or lease of land, and various other uses.

Online contracts have become common. E-signature laws have made the electronic contract and signature as legally valid as a paper contract. Certain sections in information Technology Act (2000) also provide for validity of online contract.

Classification of Contracts

There are many different types of contracts, which may take numerous forms:

1. Oral or Written

Usually, a contract doesn't have to be in writing. As long as the parties sufficiently indicate that they intend to make a contract, oral promises are enforceable.

There are some kinds of contracts, however, that must be in writing to be enforceable. These are the promises governed by **the Statute of Frauds**. The Statute listed a number of kinds of contracts in which the problem of fraud was thought to be especially acute, and required that there be written evidence of the agreement to make the contract enforceable.

2. Bilateral or Unilateral

In discussing **bilateral** and **unilateral** contracts, we are concerned with the promises of the parties. In a bilateral contract, both parties to the contract have promised to do something. This exchange of promises results in a bilateral contract.

Some contractual situations involve a promise in exchange for some requested performance or forbearance to perform. Only one party to the contract makes a promise, hence it is a unilateral contract.

3. Void, Voidable, and Unenforceable

A **void** agreement is one that lacks one of the elements of a contract. A contract never comes into existence because of the absence of one of these elements, and thus to speak in terms of a "void contract" is technically a **misnomer**. The contract has never existed because of the absence of one of the elements.

A voidable contract is an agreement that contains all the elements of a contract, but for one reason or another one of the parties may be entitled to **rescind** the contract. One of the individuals may lack full contractual capacity, or there may be circumstances surrounding the execution of the agreement that would allow one of the parties to avoid the agreement at his options.

An unenforceable contract is an agreement that satisfies all the requirements of a contract but may not be enforced by a court. For instance, the Statute of Frauds requires certain types of contracts to be in writing in order to be enforceable. If there is an oral contract that falls under the Statute of Frauds, it may not be enforced in the courts despite the fact that it contains all the requirements of a contract.

The Essentials of a Valid Contract

Under the common law, a **valid** contract is an agreement that contains all of the essential elements of a contract:

1. There must be an offer and acceptance: the agreement. If there is no agreement reached by the parties, of course there is no contract and thus no so-called "valid contract."

2. There must be consideration (unless the agreement is under seal).

3. Certain types of agreement are only valid if made in a particular form, e.g., in writing.

4. The contract parties must have the intention to create legal relations.

5. The parties must have the appropriate capacity to contract.

6. There must be genuine consent by the parties to the terms of the contract, and the terms must be clear and certain.

7. The contract must not have been concluded as a result of undue influence, **duress** or **misrepresentation**.

8. The contract must not **contradict** public policy or be otherwise illegal.

9. The contract must be capable of being performed.

10. The contract must not be frustrated by an **intervening** event.

Disputes

1. Choice of Forum

Many contracts contain a clause setting out where disputes in relation to the contract should be litigated. Whether the "chosen court" will exercise jurisdiction, and whether courts not chosen will decline jurisdiction depends on the legislation of the state concerned, on whether the clause is in conformity with formal requirements (in many U.S. states a Choice of Court Agreement clause is only exclusive, when the word "exclusive" is explicitly mentioned) and the type of action. Some states will not accept action that has no connection to the court that was chosen, and others will not recognize a choice of court clause when they consider them themselves a more convenient forum.

2. Choice of Law

The law that is applicable to a contract is dependent on the conflict of laws legislation of the court where an action in relation to a contract is brought. In the absence of a choice of law clause, the law of the forum or the law with which the conflict has the strongest link is generally determined as the applicable law. A choice of law-clause is recognized in the U.S. (but generally only regarding state law, and not internationally).

New Words & Expressions

enforceable	[ɪnˈfɔːsəbl]	adj.	可强行的，可强迫的，可实施的
Uniform Commercial Code (UCC)			《统一商法典》
breach	[briːtʃ]	n.	违背；破坏；破裂；缺口
		vt.	攻破；破坏；违反
assent	[əˈsent]	vi.	赞成；赞成；赞同
		n.	同意，赞同
consideration	[kənˌsɪdəˈreɪʃn]	n.	对价
substitute	[ˈsʌbstɪtjuːt]	vt.& vi.	代替，替换，代用
		n.	代替者；替补（运动员）；替代物；[语法学]代用词
		vi.	用……替代。
consequential	[ˌkɒnsɪˈkwenʃl]	adj.	作为结果的，间接的；重要的
reliance	[rɪˈlaɪəns]	n.	依靠，依赖；信任，信赖，信心；所信赖的人或物

the Statute of Frauds			《反欺诈法》
bilateral	[ˌbaɪˈlætərəl]	adj.	双边的,双方的;两侧的;双向的;双系的
unilateral	[ˌjuːnɪˈlætrəl]	adj.	单边的,一方的;单方有义务的;片面的;仅由一方实行或承担
void	[vɔɪd]	adj.	空的,空虚的,没人住的;(职位)空缺着的;无效的
		n.	太空,宇宙空间;空位,空隙;空虚感,寂寞的心情
		vt.	使无效;宣布……作废;取消;排泄
misnomer	[mɪsˈnəʊmə(r)]	n.	使用不当的名字或名称
rescind	[rɪˈsɪnd]	vt.	废除;撤销
valid	[ˈvælɪd]	adj.	有效的;有法律效力的;正当的;健全的
duress	[djuˈres]	n.	威胁,逼迫
misrepresentation	[ˌmɪsˌreprɪzenˈteɪʃn]	n.	误传
contradict	[ˌkɒntrəˈdɪkt]	vt.	反驳,驳斥;否认;与……矛盾,与……抵触
		vi.	反驳;否认;发生矛盾
intervening	[ˌɪntəˈviːnɪŋ]	adj.	发生于其间的;介于中间的
		v.	介入(intervene 的现在分词);调停;干涉;介于……之间

Exercises

I. Choose the proper explanation to each of the follwing legal terms.

1. Uniform Commercial Code

   A. The application of the French Civil Code to commercial transactions made between the United States and France.

   B. Pricing mechanism to determine the retail commercial value of army uniforms.

   C. Mass media regulation which fixes advertising costs on American television.

D. A proposed code that has now been adopted by most of the state legislatures in the hope of creating a common commercial law in the United States.

2. Consideration

   A. Process of judicial deliberation before rendering a decision in a contested case.

   B. The lengthy recitals of boilerplate language appearing in many contracts.

   C. The inducement to enter a contract, and a necessary element to prove the validity of a contract.

   D. The detrimental reliance of an offeree.

3. Breach of contract

   A. Excused failure to fulfill a promise.

   B. The failure, without any legal excuse to perform part or all of a contract.

   C. Party's unreasonable fear that the other party will not be able to fulfill a promise in the future.

   D. The oral agreement of the parties to modify the terms of a written contract.

4. Statute of Frauds

   A. Codification of the equitable doctrine of quantum meruit.

   B. The statute providing criminal sanctions for fraud.

   C. The statute providing civil remedies for tort of fraud.

   D. The statute providing that certain agreements are so important that they must be in writing and signed to avoid fraud.

5. Rescind

   A. To transmit a document to another party a second time, particularly by the use of an inexpensive fax machine.

   B. To undo or to repudiate a contract, so that the parties are effectively restored to the positions that had before they entered into the contract.

   C. The intentional failure to incorporate all of the material terms from a business negotiation in the final contract.

   D. The intentional omission of uncertain terms from a contract due to anticipated fluctuations in the market price of manufacturing a product.

II. Choose the proper words from the list below to fill in the blanks. Change the form of the words if necessary.

> remedy / binding / adequate / enforce / consideration
> benefit / agreement / damages / assurance / mutual

Contract is a(n) ____1____ creating obligations enforceable by law. The basic elements of a contract are ____2____ assent, consideration, capacity, and legality. In some states, the element of consideration can be satisfied by a valid substitute. Possible remedies for breach of contract include general damages, consequential ____3____, reliance damages, and specific performance. Specifically speaking, contracts are promises that the law will ____4____. The law provides ____5____ if a promise is breached or recognizes the performance of a promise as a duty. Contracts arise when a duty does or may come into existence, because of a promise made by one of the parties. To be legally ____6____ as a contract, a promise must be exchanged for adequate ____7____. Adequate consideration is a ____8____ or detriment which a party receives which reasonably and fairly induces them to make the promise/contract. For example, promises that are purely gifts are not considered enforceable because the personal satisfaction the grantor of the promise may receive from the act of giving is normally not considered ____9____ consideration. Certain promises that are not considered contracts may, in limited circumstances, be enforced if one party has relied to his detriment on the ____10____ of the other party.

UNIT 23
TORTS

A tort, in common law jurisdictions, is a civil wrong that unfairly causes someone else to suffer loss or harm resulting in legal liability for the person who commits the **tortious** act, called a **tortfeasor**. For example, if you punch your neighbor in the nose, run over a **pedestrian** by driving carelessly, or injure a customer by serving burning hot coffee, you have committed a tort. Although crimes may be torts, the cause of legal action is not necessarily a crime, as the harm may be due to negligence which does not amount to criminal negligence. The victim of the harm can recover their loss as damages in a lawsuit. Tort law is still the source of most civil suits in the United States.

Tort law is different from criminal law in that:

➢ Torts may result from negligent as well as intentional or criminal actions.

➢ Tort lawsuits have a lower burden of proof such as **preponderance** of evidence rather than beyond a reasonable doubt.

Sometimes a plaintiff may prevail in a tort case even if the person who **allegedly** caused harm was acquitted in an earlier criminal trial. For example, O. J. Simpson was acquitted in criminal court of murder but later found liable for the tort of wrongful death.

Types of Torts

Legal injuries are not limited to physical injuries and may include emotional, economic, or reputational injuries as well as violations of privacy, property, or constitutional rights. Torts comprise such varied topics as auto accidents, false imprisonment, defamation, product liability, copyright infringement, and environmental pollution (toxic torts). While many torts are the result of **negligence**, tort law also recognizes intentional torts, where a person has intentionally acted in a way that harms another, and in a few cases (particularly for product liability in the United States) "strict liability" which allows recovery without the need to demonstrate negligence. So tort law is divided into three categories: intentional torts, negligence, and strict liability. There are also separate areas of tort law including nuisance, and strict liability. There are also separate areas of tort law including **nuisance**, **defamation**, invasion of privacy, and a category of economic torts (a bundle of torts including fraud, negligent misrepresentation, interference with contractual relations, interference with prospective advantage, and **injurious** falsehood).

1. Intentional Torts

Intentional torts are intentional actions that result in harm to the plaintiff. The harm need not be intended, but the act must be intentional, not merely careless or reckless. Most intentional torts are also crimes. The most common intentional tort is **battery**. The legal standard for a battery is an intentional, unconsented touching. (Batteries such as shootings, stabbings, and beatings are also criminal law violations.) Although battery is commonly linked with **assault** and assault is the act of putting a person in fear of bodily harm. Battery occurs only if there is an actual physical contact.

2. Negligence

Negligence is a failure to exercise the care that a reasonably **prudent** person would exercise in like circumstances. The area of tort law known as negligence involves harm caused by carelessness, not intentional harm. The behavior usually consists of actions, but can also consist of omissions when there is some duty to act.

Through civil litigation, if an injured person proves that another person acted negligently to cause their injury, they can recover damages to compensate for their harm. Proving a case for negligence can potentially entitle the injured plaintiff to compensation for harm to their body, property, mental well-being, financial status, or intimate relationships. However, because negligence cases are very fact-specific, this general definition does not fully explain the concept of when the law will require one person to compensate another for losses caused by accidental injury. Further, the law of negligence at common law is only one aspect of the law of liability. Although resulting damages must be proven in order to recover compensation in a negligence action, the nature and extent of those damages are not the primary focus of negligence cases.

3. Strict liability

In tort law, strict liability is the imposition of liability on a party without a finding of fault (such as negligence or tortious intent). The claimant need only prove that the tort occurred and that the defendant was responsible. The law imputes strict liability to situations it considers to be inherently dangerous. It discourages reckless behavior and needless loss by forcing potential defendants to take every possible **precaution**. It also has the effect of simplifying and thereby expediting court decisions in these cases.

A classic example of strict liability is the owner of a tiger **rehabilitation** center. No matter how strong the tiger cages are, if an animal escapes and causes damage and injury, the owner is held liable. Another example is a contractor hiring a **demolition subcontractor** that lacks proper insurance. If the subcontractor makes a mistake, the contractor is strictly liable for any damage that occurs. A more everyday example is that of a passenger on public transport who was unable to purchase a valid ticket for the journey due to **extraneous** circumstances, such as being unable to purchase a ticket for whatever reason. Under strict liability it does not matter if the ticket machine was broken, or the train was early, or there were no staff at the counter. The legal responsibility for holding a valid ticket falls on the passenger and the passenger should not have travelled without one regardless of the circumstances.

In strict liability situations, although the plaintiff does not have to prove fault, the defendant can raise a defense of absence of fault, especially in cases of product liability, where the defense may argue that the defect was the result of the plaintiff's actions and not of the product, that is, no inference of defect should be drawn solely because an accident occurs. If the plaintiff can prove that the defendant knew about the defect before the damages occurred, additional **punitive** damages can be awarded to the victim in some jurisdictions.

Remedies

The main remedy against tortious loss is compensation in damages or money. In a limited range of cases, tort law will tolerate self-help, such as reasonable force to expel a **trespasser**. This is a defense against the tort of battery. Further, in the case of a continuing tort, or even where harm is merely threatened, the courts will sometimes grant an **injunction**. This means a command, for something other than money by the court, such as restraining the continuance or threat of harm. Usually injunctions will not impose positive obligations on tortfeasors, but some Australian jurisdictions can make an order for specific performance to ensure that the defendant carries out their legal obligations, especially in relation to nuisance matters.

New Words & Expressions

tortuous	[ˈtɔːtʃuəs]	adj.	侵权行为的，侵权行为性质的
tortfeasor	[ˈtɔtˈfizə(r)]	n.	犯侵权行为者
pedestrian	[pəˈdestrɪən]	n.	步行者；行人
		adj.	徒步的；平淡无奇的；一般的
preponderance	[prɪˈpɒndərəns]	n.	数量上的优势
allegedly	[əˈledʒɪdlɪ]	adv.	依其申述；据说
negligence	[ˈneɡlɪdʒəns]	n.	疏忽；[法]过失；粗心大意
nuisance	[ˈnjuːsns]	n.	讨厌的东西(人，行为)麻烦事；非法妨害，损害；麻烦事
defamation	[ˌdefəˈmeɪʃn]	n.	诽谤，中伤
injurious	[ɪnˈdʒʊərɪəs]	adj.	伤害的；中伤的；不公正的
battery	[ˈbætrɪ]	n.	[法]殴打
assault	[əˈsɔːlt]	n.	攻击；袭击，进攻；威胁，殴打；侵犯人身
		vt.	袭击；强暴；使(感官)难受
		vi.	发起攻击；动武

prudent	[ˈpruːdnt]	adj.	小心的，慎重的；精明的，节俭的；顾虑周到的，稳健的；世故的，精明的
precaution	[prɪˈkɔːʃn]	n.	预防，防备，警惕；预防措施
		vt.	使提防；预先警告
rehabilitation	[ˌriːəˌbɪlɪˈteɪʃn]	n.	修复；复兴；复职；恢复名誉
demolition	[ˌdeməˈlɪʃn]	n.	毁坏，破坏，拆毁；(pl.) 炸药
subcontractor	[ˌsʌbkənˈtræktə(r)]	n.	转包商，次承包者
extraneous	[ɪkˈstreɪniəs]	adj.	外部的；外来的；无关的；不相干的
punitive	[ˈpjuːnətɪv]	adj.	处罚的，惩罚性的；令人受苦的
trespasser	[ˈtrespəsə(r)]	n.	侵害者，违反者，侵入者
injunction	[ɪnˈdʒʌŋkʃn]	n.	命令，禁令，强制令

Exercises

I. Choose the proper explanation to each of the following legal terms.

1. Tort

    A. A cake in Germany or Austria, or a sandwich in Mexico.

    B. A breach of contract punishable by imprisonment.

    C. A civil wrong or private injury not based on contract law.

    D. An involuntary action which amounts to a criminal offense because of an actual or potential injury.

2. Elements of a tort

    A. The requirements that a defendant must prove to exculpate himself from liability for a civil wrong.

    B. The parts of a prima facie cause of action.

    C. The statutory codification of a common law tort.

    D. Malpractice insurance.

3. Assault

   A. A mineral from the Dead Sea.

   B. A military invasion.

   C. The civil wrong of inflicting actual bodily injury on another.

   D. The act of putting a person in reasonable apprehension (fear) of imminent (immediate) bodily injury.

4. Intent

   A. An action required to sustain a tort.

   B. Strict liability.

   C. The desire to cause a certain result or to act with substantial knowledge that an injury will result.

   D. Where desert nomads live.

5. Negligence

   A. Forgetfulness.

   B. Willful and wanton misconduct.

   C. An intentional tort that can be brought for "wrongful birth" or for "wrongful death."

   D. A tort that will impose liability for a breach of a duty that proximately causes an injury.

II. Choose the proper words from the list below to fill in the blanks. Change the form of the words if necessary.

> malicious / defendants / gravity / liability / civil
> litigation / property / plaintiff / punitive / compensate

Tort law is a form of ____1____ law where private parties use the legal system to resolve disputes among themselves. A tort is an omission or a wrongful act against a person or his ____2____. Here, the word "wrongful" implies a violation of one person's legal duty to another. Every tort shares three elements: (1) A legal duty owed by the defendant to the ____3____; (2) A breach of that duty; (3) Damage caused to the plaintiff as a result. The purpose of tort ____4____ is to require a wrongdoer or the party at fault to ____5____ a victim for the injury incurred (compensatory damages). Compensatory damages in a typical tort case usually include: (1) medical expenses; (2) lost income form earnings; (3) property damages; (4) pain and suffering, and (5) loss of life or limb. These losses include those actually sustained in the past and those estimated in the future. There is also another kind of damages called ____6____ damages, or exemplary damages, which are awarded to punish ____7____ for committing intentional torts and for negligent behavior considered "gross" or "willful and wanton." For an award of punitive damages, the defendant's motive must be "____8____," "fraudulent," or "evil." Increasingly, punitive damages are also awarded for dangerously negligent conduct that shows a conscious disregard for the interests of others. These damages are used to deter future wrongdoing. Torts may be classified according to the ____9____ of the fault of the wrongdoer. By this way of classification, these are three types of torts: intentional torts, torts of negligence and strict liability torts. Intentional torts are those wrongs in which the persons charges have acted in such a manner that they either wanted to harm someone or knew that what they did would result in harm. Negligence is the unintentional causing of harm that could have been prevented if the defendant had acted as a reasonable and prudent person. Strict liability tort is a new area of tort law. It assigns ____10____ regardless of fault as a matter of social policy.

UNIT 24
PROPERTY LAW

The word property, in everyday usage, refers to an object (or objects) owned by a person and the relationship the person has to it. In law, the concept acquires a more **nuanced** rendering. Factors to consider include the nature of the object, the relationship between the person and the object, the relationship between a number of people in relation to the object, and how the object is regarded within the prevailing political system. Most broadly and concisely, property in the legal sense refers to the rights of people in or over certain objects or things. Property law is the area of law that governs the various forms of ownership and tenancy in real property (land as distinct from personal or movable possessions) and in personal property, within the common law legal system.

Acquisition of Property

1. Find

(1) Abandoned Property

Abandoned property refers to personal property left by an owner who intentionally **relinquishes** all rights to its control. Real property may not be abandoned. At common law, a person who finds abandoned property may claim it. To do so, the finder must take definite steps to show their claim.

(2) Lost Property

Lost property is personal property that was unintentionally left by its true owner. At common law, a person who found lost personal property could keep it until and unless the original owner comes forward. This rule applied to people who discovered lost property in public areas, as well as to people who discovered lost property on their property. Real property may not be lost.

2. Adverse Possession

Adverse possession is a doctrine, under which a person in possession of land owned by someone else may acquire valid title to it, so long as certain common law requirements are met, and the adverse possessor is in possession for a sufficient period of time, as defined by a statute of limitations.

(1) The common law requirements

The common law requirements have evolved over time, and the **articulation** of those requirements varies somewhat from jurisdiction to jurisdiction.

(2) The statute of limitations

A typical statute will require possession for 7 years, if under color of title, or 20 years, if not.

3. Will, Trust, and **Intestate Succession**

(1) Will and Make a Living Will

A will is a formal expression of intent regarding the distribution of one's property at death. The person who makes the will is called the **testator** (or in older usage, in the case of a woman, the **testatrix**). A regular will concern the treatment of one's property after the death; a living will concerns the treatment of a person while he is still alive.

(2) Trust

A trust is an arrangement where one person or institution, the trustee holds, manages, and distributes assets for the benefits of another, the beneficiary. A **testamentary** trust is one created by will—specifically, by a clause that gives all or part of the estate to a designated trustee to be held for the benefit of specified beneficiaries. There are many other devices besides wills and trusts for transferring wealth at death, including joint accounts, life insurance, and **IRAs** with named beneficiaries.

(3) Intestate Succession

Each state has laws of intestate succession that dictate who will inherit one's property if one dies without a will. Generally, it goes to our spouse, children, or closest blood relatives. If no surviving relative who qualifies under the statute can be found, the property goes to the state—a process called escheat.

4. **Bailment**

A bailment is a non-ownership transfer of possession. Under English Common Law, the right to possess a thing is separate and distinct from owning the thing. In some jurisdictions, an owner of an object can steal his own property, a curious result of the distinction. When a bailment is created, the article is said to have been bailed. One who delivers the article is the **bailor**. One who receives a bailed article is **bailee**.

Property Rights

Property rights are rights over things enforceable against all other persons. By contrast, contractual rights are rights enforceable against particular persons. Property rights may, however, arise from a contract; the two systems of rights overlap. In relation to the sale of land, for example, two sets of legal relationships exist alongside one another: the contractual right to sue for damages, and the property right exercisable over the land. More minor property rights may be created by contract, as in the case of easements, covenants, and equitable servitudes.

A separate distinction is evident where the rights granted are insufficiently substantial to confer on the nonowner a definable interest or right in the thing. The clearest example of these rights is the license. In general, even if licenses are created by a binding contract, they do not give rise to property interests.

Possession

The concept of possession developed from a legal system whose principal concern was to avoid civil disorder. The general principle is that a person in possession of land or goods, even as a wrongdoer, is entitled to take action against anyone interfering with the possession unless the person interfering is able to demonstrate a superior right to do so. In England, the Torts (Interference with Goods) Act 1977 has significantly amended the law relating to wrongful interference with goods and abolished some longstanding remedies and doctrines.

Transfer of Property

The most usual way of acquiring an interest in property is as the result of a consensual transaction with the previous owner, for example, a sale or a gift. **Dispositions** by will may also be regarded as consensual transactions, since the effect of a will is to provide for the distribution of the deceased person's property to nominated beneficiaries. A person may also obtain an interest in property under a trust established for his or her benefit by the owner of the property.

It is also possible for property to pass from one person to another independently of the consent of the property owner. For example, this occurs when a person dies intestate, goes bankrupt, or has the property taken in execution of a court judgment.

Priority

Different parties may claim an interest in property by mistake or fraud, with the claims being inconsistent of each other. For example, the party creating or transferring an interest may have a valid title, but intentionally or negligently creates several interests wholly or partially inconsistent with each other. A court resolves the dispute by **adjudicating** the priorities of the interests.

New Words & Expressions

nuanced	['nju:a:nst]	adj.	有细微差别的
relinquish	[rɪ'lɪŋkwɪʃ]	vt.	放弃；让出（权利，财产等）；放开，松手；撤离
adverse possession			违法占有，无合法所有权之占有
articulation	[ɑ:ˌtɪkju'leɪʃn]	n.	清晰度，咬合，关节；发音；接合
intestate succession			无遗嘱继承
testator	[tes'teɪtə]	n.	（尤指死者）留有遗嘱的人
testatrix	[tes'teɪtrɪks]	n.	立遗嘱的女人
testamentary	[ˌtestə'mentərɪ]	adj.	遗嘱的,据遗嘱的,遗嘱中有的
IRAs		abbr.	Individual Retirement Accounts 个人退休账户

UNIT 24
PROPERTY LAW

bailment	['beɪlmənt]	n.	（通常指某一特定目的的）财产寄托
bailor	['beɪlɔr]	n.	财物（财产等）寄托人
bailee	[beɪ'li:]	n.	（如扣留或修理财物的）受托人
disposition	[ˌdɪspə'zɪʃn]	n.	性情，性格；意向，倾向；安排，配置
priority	[praɪ'ɒrətɪ]	n.	优先，优先权
adjudicate	[ə'dʒu:dɪkeɪt]	vt.	判决，宣判；当……的评判员（或裁判员、仲裁人）
		n.	判决，宣判；裁判员

Exercises

I. Choose the proper words from the list below to fill in the blanks. Change the form of the words if necessary.

> easement / lien / nuisance / property / intellectual property rights
> adverse possession / infringement / leasehold / bailment / concurrent estate

1. The protection of industrial _____ has as its object patents, utility models, industrial designs, trademarks, service marks, trade names, indications of source or appellations of origin, and the repression of unfair competition.

2. In considering such requests, the need for proportionality between the seriousness of the _____ and the remedies ordered as well as the interests of third parties shall be taken into account.

3. Protection and enforcement of all _____ shall meet the objectives to contribute to the promotion of technological innovation and to the transfer and dissemination of technology, to the mutual advantage of producers and users of technological knowledge and in a manner conducive to social and economic welfare, and to a balance of rights and obligations.

4. An estate in land in which two or more parties have a contemporaneous interest in the same realty is a _____.

5. A _____ is an estate in land. The tenant has a present possessory interest in the leased premises, and the landlord has a future interest. Certain rights and liabilities flow from this property relationship between landlord and tenant.

6. _____ means any mortgage, charge, pledge, hypothecation, security, interest, assignment, encumbrance, title retention agreement or arrangement, restrictive covenant or other encumbrance of any nature or any other arrangement or condition that in substance secures payment or performance of an obligation.

7. The holder of a(n) _____, which is either affirmative or negative, appurtenant or in gross, has the right to use a tract of land for a special purpose, but has no right to possess and enjoy the tract of land.

8. Title of real property may be acquired by _____. Gaining title by it results from the operation of the statute of limitations for trespass to real property.

9. _____ is the act of placing property in the custody and control of another, usually by agreement in which the holder (bailee) is responsible for the safekeeping and return of the property.

10. There are two types of _____, i.e., "private" and "public". The former is one that unreasonably interferes with the use and enjoyment of nearby property; the latter is a species of call-all criminal offense, consisting of an interference with the rights of the community at large, which may include anything from the obstruction of a highway to public gaming-house or indecent exposure.

II. Choose the proper words from the list below to fill in the blanks. Change the form of the words if necessary.

> voluntarily / consideration / parties / agreement / enforce
> obligations / liable / promises / offering / contract

Contract law has come to us from common law and it is said that it is an offspring of tort law. Both contracts and torts give rise to ____1____. But tort obligations (i.e., the obligation to indemnify for your negligence) are imposed by the law; it is not normally a choice one makes. Contracts, on the other hand, are a vehicle by which persons ____2____ create obligations upon themselves. In some circumstances, you can ____3____ your way out of tort liability. For example, the owner of a sporting event stadium or a concert hall may have a disclaimer on the back of your ticket (a tiny contract but a contract nonetheless) which says that they cannot be held ____4____ for any accidents on the premises. This is an attempt to contract out of tort liability. In addition, tort liability does not require ____5____. It should also be said that the existence of a contract does not necessarily relieve a person of liability under tort law between the contracting ____6____, unless the contract specifically says so. ____7____ are what contracts are all about. A contract is made up of a promise of one person to do a certain thing in exchange for a promise from another person to do another thing. Contract law exists to make sure that people keep their promises and that if they do not, the law will ____8____ it upon them. Contract law is based on several Latin legal principles, the most important of which is consensus ad idem, which means a meeting of the minds between the parties or, in other words, a clear understanding, ____9____ and acceptance of each person's contribution. Lawyers say that it is from the moment of "consensus ad idem" that a contract is formed and may be enforced by the courts. So a contract requires a(n) ____10____ between the parties. But not all agreements are contracts. Non-business, religious, or charitable agreements are not always contracts. The same has been said of family or household agreements (in one case, a casual arrangement between friends to share hockey tickets was held not to be a contract: ***Eng v. Evans, 83 Alta. L.R. (2d) 107 (ABQB, 1991))***.

UNIT 25
EVIDENCE LAW

The law of evidence **encompasses** the rules and legal principles that govern the proof of facts in a legal proceeding. These rules determine what evidence must or must not be considered by the trier of fact in reaching its decision and, sometimes, the weight that may be given to that evidence. The law of evidence is also concerned with the **quantum** (amount), quality, and type of proof needed to prevail in litigation. The quantum of evidence is the amount of evidence needed; the quality of proof is how reliable such evidence should be considered. This includes such concepts as **hearsay**, **authentication**, **admissibility**, reasonable doubt, and clear and convincing evidence.

There are several types of evidence, depending on the form or source. Evidence governs the use of **testimony** (e.g., oral or written statements, such as an **affidavit**), exhibits (e.g., physical objects), documentary material, or demonstrative evidence, which are admissible (i.e., allowed to be considered by the trier of fact, such as jury) in a judicial or administrative proceeding (e.g. a court of law).

The Features of Evidence

1. Admissibility

In trial practice, the process by which a party attempting to have some sort of evidence admitted at trial must provide sufficient evidence so that a reasonable juror can conclude that the evidence the party seeks to admit is what that party claims it to be. The process of authentication is often referred to as "laying a foundation" for the evidence desired to be admitted at trial. There are several different methods that can be used to authenticate evidence, including testimony by a witness with personal knowledge on the authenticity of the evidence. With regards to contracts or other documents, it is safe to sign or to execute the document.

2. Relevance

In every jurisdiction based on the English common law tradition, evidence must conform to a number of rules and restrictions to be admissible. Evidence must be relevant— that is, it must be directed at proving or disproving a legal element. However the relevance of evidence is ordinarily a necessary condition but a sufficient condition for the admissibility of evidence. For example, relevant evidence may be excluded if it is unfairly prejudicial, confusing, or the relevance of evidence cannot be determined by **syllogistic** reasoning — if/ then logic — alone.

Two Types of Evidence

1. Direct Evidence

Direct evidence supports the truth of an **assertion** (in criminal law, an assertion of guilt or of innocence) directly, i.e., without an **intervening** inference. In direct evidence a witness relates what he or she directly experienced. (Usually the experience is by sight or hearing, though it may come through any sense, including smell, touch or pain.)

2. Circumstantial Evidence

Circumstantial evidence is evidence that relies on an inference to connect it to a conclusion of fact—like a fingerprint at the scene of a crime. On its own, circumstantial evidence allows for more than one explanation. Different pieces of circumstantial evidence may be required, so that each **corroborates** the conclusions drawn from the others. Together, they may more strongly support one particular inference over another. An explanation involving circumstantial evidence becomes more likely once alternative explanations have been ruled out.

Burdens of Proof

Different types of proceedings require parties to meet different burdens of proof, the typical examples being beyond a reasonable doubt, clear and convincing evidence, and **preponderance** of the evidence. Many jurisdictions have burden-shifting provisions, which require that if one party produces evidence tending to prove a certain point, the burden shifts to the other party to produce superior evidence tending to disprove it.

One special category of information in this area includes things of which the court may take judicial notice. This category covers matters that are so well known that the court may deem them proved without the introduction of any evidence. In a civil case, where the court takes judicial notice of the fact, that fact is deemed conclusively proved. In a criminal case, however, the defense may always submit evidence to **rebut** a point for which judicial notice has been taken.

Exclusion of Evidence

Public policy doctrines for the exclusion of relevant evidence, in the law of evidence in the United States, encompass several types of evidence that would be relevant to prove facts at issue in a legal proceeding, but which is nonetheless excluded because of public policy concerns. There are five major areas of exclusion that arise out of the Federal Rules of Evidence ("FRE"): subsequent remedial measures, ownership of liability insurance, offers to plead guilty to a crime, offers to settle a claim, and offers to pay medical expenses. Many states have modified versions of the FRE under their own state evidence codes which widen or narrow the public policy exclusions in state courts.

The exclusionary rule, under which evidence gathered by the police from an illegal search is excluded, is of similar operation but is typically considered separately.

Authentication

Certain kinds of evidence, such as documentary evidence, are subject to the requirement that the offeror provide the trial judge with a certain amount of evidence (which need not be much and it need not be very strong) suggesting that the offered item of tangible evidence (e.g. a document, a gun) is what the offeror claims it is. This authentication requirement has import primarily in jury trials. If evidence of authenticity is lacking in a bench trial, the trial judge will simply dismiss the evidence as unpersuasive or irrelevant.

Hearsay

Hearsay is one of the largest and most complex areas of the law of evidence in common-law jurisdictions. The default rule is that hearsay evidence is inadmissible. Hearsay is an out of court statement offered to prove the truth of the matter asserted. A party is offering a statement to prove the truth of the matter asserted if the party is trying to prove that the assertion made by the declarant (the maker of the out-of-trial statement) is true. For example, prior to trial Bob says, "Jane went to the store." If the party offering this statement as evidence at trial is trying to prove that Jane actually went to the store, the statement is being offered to prove the truth of the matter asserted. However, at both common law and under evidence codifications such as the Federal Rules of Evidence, there are dozens of exemptions from and exceptions to the hearsay rule.

New Words & Expressions

encompass	[ɪnˈkʌmpəs]	vt.	围绕, 包围; 包含或包括某事物; 完成
quantum	[ˈkwɒntəm]	n.	[物]量子; 定量, 总量
hearsay	[ˈhɪəseɪ]	n.	传闻, 道听途说; 小道消息; 谣传; 风言风语
authentication	[ɔːˌθentɪˈkeɪʃn]	n.	证明, 鉴定; 身份验证; 认证; 密押
admissibility	[ədˌmɪsəˈbɪlətɪ]	n.	可容许, 有入场的资格; 可允许性; 可容许性
testimony	[ˈtestɪmənɪ]	n.	(法庭上证人的)证词; 证明, 证据; 表示, 表明; 声明, 宣言
affidavit	[ˌæfəˈdeɪvɪt]	n.	〈法〉宣誓口供; 宣誓书
syllogistic	[ˌsɪləˈdʒɪstɪk]	adj.	三段论法的, 演绎的, 演绎性的
assertion	[əˈsɜːʃn]	n.	主张; 声称; 使用; 明确肯定
intervening	[ˌɪntəˈviːnɪŋ]	adj.	发生于其间的; 介于中间的
		v.	干涉; 介入(intervene 的现在分词); 调停; 介于……之间
corroborate	[kəˈrɒbəreɪt]	vt.	证实, 支持(某种说法、信仰、理论等); 使(信仰等)坚定; 使巩固
		n.	确证者, 证物

| preponderance | [prɪˈpɒndərəns] | n. | 数量上的优势。 |
| rebut | [rɪˈbʌt] | vt. | 反驳，驳回；击退。 |

Exercises

I. Choose the proper words from the list below to fill in the blanks. Change the form of the words if necessary.

> duress / admissibility / authentication / competent / foundation
> exclusionary / demonstrative / relevant / existence / defendant

There are four traditional types of evidence: real, ____1____, documentary, and testimonial. Some rules of evidence apply to all four types and some apply only to some or one of them. The basic prerequisites of ____2____ are relevance, materiality, and competence. In general, if evidence is shown to be relevant, material, and competent, and is not barred by an ____3____ rule, it is admissible. Evidence is ____4____ when it has any tendency in reason to make the fact that it is offered to prove or disprove either more or less probable. Evidence is material if it is offered to prove a fact that is at issue in the case. Evidence is ____5____ if the proof that is being offered meets certain traditional requirements of reliability. The preliminary showing that the evidence meets those tests, and any other prerequisites of admissibility, is called the foundational evidence.

Real evidence is a thing the ____6____ or characteristics of which are relevant and material. It is usually a thing that was directly involved in some event in the case. The written contract upon which an action is based is real evidence both to prove its terms and that it was executed by the ____7____. If it is written in a faltering and unsteady hand, it may also be relevant to show that the writer was under ____8____ at the time of its execution. The bloody bloomers, the murder weapon, a crumpled automobile, the scene of an accident — all may be real evidence. To be admissible, real evidence, like all evidence, must be relevant, material, and competent. Establishing these basic prerequisites, and any other special ones that may apply, is called laying a _____9_____. The relevance and materiality of real evidence are usually obvious. Its competence is established by showing that it really is what it is supposed to be. Proving that real or other evidence is what it purports to be is called ____10____.

II. Translate the following sentences into Chinese.
1. Evidence is any statement or material object from which reasonable conclusions can be drawn.
2. Evidence in a criminal trial concerns the intent, motive, means and opportunity to commit a crime.
3. Circumstantial evidence consists of information gleaned from witnesses and documents that point to an individual as the perpetrator of a crime.
4. It is the work of forensic scientists to examine the physical evidence, and using the methods of science, to reconstruct the events that constituted the crime.
5. Expert witnesses are allowed to draw inferences from facts which the judge or jury is not competent to draw.

UNIT 26
INTELLECTUAL PROPERTY LAW

Intellectual property (IP) is a term referring to creations of the intellect for which a monopoly is assigned to designated owners by law. Some common types of intellectual property rights (IPR) are trademarks, copyright, patents, industrial design rights, and in some jurisdictions trade secrets: all these cover music, literature, and other artistic works; discoveries and inventions; and words, phrases, symbols, and designs.

While intellectual property law has evolved over centuries, it was not until the 19th century that the term intellectual property began to be used, and not until the late 20th century that it became commonplace in the majority of the world.

Intellectual Property Rights

Intellectual property rights include patents, copyright, industrial design rights, trademarks, plant variety rights, trade dress, and in some jurisdictions trade secrets.

1. Patents

A patent is a form of right granted by the government to an inventor, giving the owner the right to exclude others from making, using, selling, offering to sell, and importing an invention for a limited period of time, in exchange for the public disclosure of the invention. An invention is a solution to a specific technological problem, which may be a product or a process and generally has to fulfill three main requirements: it has to be new, not obvious and there needs to be an industrial applicability.

2. Copyright

A copyright gives the creator of original work exclusive rights to it, usually for a limited time. Copyright may apply to a wide range of creative, intellectual, or artistic forms, or "works." Copyright does not cover ideas and information themselves, only the form or manner in which they are expressed.

Copyright may apply to a wide range of creative, intellectual, or artistic forms, or "works." Specifics vary by jurisdiction, but these can include poems, theses, plays and other literary works, motion pictures, **choreography**, musical compositions, sound recordings, paintings, drawings, sculptures, photographs, computer software, radio and television broadcasts, and industrial designs. Graphic designs and industrial designs may have separate or overlapping laws applied to them in some jurisdictions.

3. Industrial Design Rights

An industrial design right (sometimes called "design right") protects the visual design of objects that are not purely **utilitarian**. An industrial design consists of the creation of a shape, **configuration** or composition of pattern or color, or combination of pattern and color in **three-dimensional** form containing **aesthetic** value. An industrial design can be a two- or three-dimensional pattern used to produce a product, industrial commodity or handicraft.

4. Trademarks

A trademark, trade mark, or trade-mark is a recognizable sign, design, or expression which identifies products or services of a particular source from those of others, although trademarks used to identify services are usually called service marks. The trademark owner can be an individual, business organization, or any legal entity. A trademark may be located on a package, a label, a voucher, or on the product itself. For the sake of corporate identity, trademarks are being displayed on company buildings.

5. Trade Dress

Trade dress is a legal term of art that generally refers to characteristics of the visual appearance of a product or its packaging (or even the design of a building) that signify the source of the product to consumers.

6. Trade Secrets

A trade secret is a formula, practice, process, design, instrument, pattern, or compilation of information which is not generally known or reasonably ascertainable, by which a business can obtain an economic advantage over competitors or customers.

Objectives of Intellectual Property Law

The stated objective of most intellectual property law (with the exception of trademarks) is to "Promote progress." By exchanging limited exclusive rights for disclosure of inventions and creative works, society and the **patentee**/copyright owner mutually benefit, and an **incentive** is created for inventors and authors to create and disclose their work. Some **commentators** have noted that the objective of intellectual property legislators and those who support its implementation appears to be "absolute protection." "If some intellectual property is desirable because it encourages innovation, they reason, more is better. The thinking is that creators will not have sufficient incentive to invent unless they are legally entitled to capture the full social value of their inventions." This absolute protection or full value view treats intellectual property as another type of "real" property, typically adopting its law and rhetoric. Other recent developments in intellectual property law, such as the America Invents Act, stress international **harmonization**. Recently there has also been much debate over the desirability of using intellectual property rights to protect cultural heritage, including intangible ones, as well as over risks of **commodification** derived from this possibility. The issue still remains open in legal scholarship.

Infringement, Misappropriation, and Enforcement

Violation of intellectual property rights, called "infringement" with respect to patents, copyright, and trademarks, and "misappropriation" with respect to trade secrets, may be a breach of civil law or criminal law, depending on the type of intellectual property involved, jurisdiction, and the nature of the action.

Patent infringement typically is caused by using or selling a patented invention without permission from the patent holder. The scope of the patented invention or the extent of protection is defined in the claims of the granted patent. There is safe harbor in many jurisdictions to use a patented invention for research. This safe harbor does not exist in the U.S. unless the research is done for purely philosophical purposes, or in order to gather data in order to prepare an application for regulatory approval of a drug.

Copyright infringement is reproducing, distributing, displaying or performing a work, or to make **derivative** works, without permission from the copyright holder, which is typically a publisher or other business representing or assigned by the work's creator. It is often called "piracy." While copyright is created the instance a work is fixed, generally the copyright holder can only get money damages if the owner registers the copyright. Enforcement of copyright is generally the responsibility of the copyright holder.

Trademark infringement occurs when one party uses a trademark that is identical or confusingly similar to a trademark owned by another party, in relation to products or services which are identical or similar to the products or services of the other party. In many countries, a trademark receives protection without registration, but **registering** a trademark provides legal advantages for enforcement. Infringement can be addressed by civil litigation and, in several jurisdictions, under criminal law.

New Words & Expressions

choreography	[ˌkɒrɪˈɒɡrəfɪ]	n.	编舞艺术；舞蹈编排
utilitarian	[ˌjuːtɪlɪˈteərɪən]	adj.	功利的；功利主义的, 实利主义的；有效用的；实用的
		n.	功利主义者；实用主义者
configuration	[kənˌfɪɡəˈreɪʃn]	n.	布局, 构造；配置
three-dimensional	[θriː dɪˈmenʃənəl]	adj.	三维的；立体的；空间的；三度
aesthetic	[iːsˈθetɪk]	adj.	审美的；美的, 美学的；有关美的；具有审美趣味的
		n.	审美观；美学标准, 美感
patentee	[ˌpætnˈtiː]	n.	专利权所有人
incentive	[ɪnˈsentɪv]	n.	动机；刺激；诱因；鼓励

		adj.	刺激性的；鼓励性质的
commentator	[ˈkɒmənteɪtə(r)]	n.	（电台的）时事评论员，实况广播报道员；注解者，注释者；评论员，解说员；主持
harmonization	[ˌhɑːmənaɪˈzeɪʃn]	n.	和谐，协调，相称；配和声
commodification	[kə,mɔdɪfɪˈkeɪʃən]	n.	商品化
infringement	[ɪnˈfrɪndʒmənt]	n.	侵权；违反；违背
misappropriation	[ˌmɪsəˌprəʊprɪˈeɪʃn]	n.	[经]侵吞，挪用，滥用；私吞
enforcement	[ɪnˈfɔːsmənt]	n.	强制，实施，执行
derivative	[dɪˈrɪvətɪv]	n.	[数]导数，微商；[化]衍生物，派生物；[语]派生词
		adj.	衍生的；导出的；拷贝的
registration	[ˌredʒɪˈstreɪʃn]	n.	登记，注册；挂号；登记（或注册、挂号）人数

Exercises

I. Judge whether the statements below are true (T) or false (F).

1. If an idea or invention is obvious, it is not patentable even if it is new and useful. (   )

2. If the infringer does not know about the patent, he is not liable for his infringement. (   )

3. When an author dies, his copyright is no longer effective. (   )

4. In order to qualify as a trademark, the mark must describe the goods in a detailed fashion. (   )

5. Even if a book is copyrighted, anyone can use the ideas in the book without the author's consent. (   )

II. Translate the following paragraph into Chinese.

A patent is an exclusive right granted by the federal government to make, use, or sell an invention for a period of seventeen years. If the patent is granted for a design the period of exclusive use cannot exceed fourteen years. The purpose of the patent laws is to advance the arts and science and to reward individuals for their inventions if an inventor does not have the exclusive right to exploit his invention for a period of time, there might be some hesitation in availing its development to the public. So, in order to encourage inventors to reveal the product of their efforts, the patent laws allow them a period of time to exclusively make, use, or sell the invention. They may also profit from this government-granted monopoly, but that is not the primary objective of the patent law. An inventor is not granted international patent protection unless allowed by the foreign country where the product is being used. Many foreign countries have laws that protect the owners of patents. International treaties have been adopted that grant patent protection to its members.

UNIT 27
CRIMINAL LAW

Criminal law or penal law is the body of law that relates to crime. It regulates social conduct and proscribes whatever is threatening, harmful, or otherwise endangering to the property, health, safety, and moral welfare of people. It includes the punishment of people who violate these laws. Criminal law varies according to jurisdiction, and differs from civil law, where emphasis is more on dispute resolution and victim compensation than on punishment. Responsibility for criminal law and criminal justice in the United States is shared between the states and the federal government.

Objectives of Criminal Law

Criminal law is distinctive for the uniquely serious potential consequences or sanctions for failure to abide by its rules. Every crime is composed of criminal elements. Capital punishment may be imposed in some jurisdictions for the most serious crimes. Physical or corporal punishment may be imposed such as whipping or caning, although these punishments are prohibited in much of the world. Individuals may be incarcerated in prison or jail in a variety of conditions depending on the jurisdiction. Confinement may be solitary. Length of incarceration may vary from a day to life. Government supervision may be imposed, including house arrest, and convicts may be required to conform to particularized guidelines as part of a parole or probation regimen. Fines also may be imposed, seizing money or property from a person convicted of a crime.

Five objectives are widely accepted for enforcement of the criminal law by punishments: **retribution**, **deterrence**, **incapacitation**, **rehabilitation** and **restoration**. Jurisdictions differ on the value to be placed on each.

UNIT 27
CRIMINAL LAW

Scope of criminal law

Many laws are enforced by threat of criminal punishment, and the range of the punishment varies with the jurisdiction. The scope of criminal law is too vast to catalog intelligently. Nevertheless, the following are some of the more typical aspects of criminal law:

1. Actus reus

Actus reus is Latin for "guilty act" and is the physical element of committing a crime. It may be accomplished by an action, by threat of action, or exceptionally, by an **omission** to act, which is a legal duty to act. For example, the act of A striking B might suffice, or a parent's failure to give food to a young child also may provide the actus reus for a crime.

2. Mens rea

Mens rea is another Latin phrase, meaning "guilty mind." This is the mental element of the crime. A guilty mind means an intention to commit some wrongful act. Intention under criminal law is separate from a person's motive.

Scope of Criminal Liability

1. **Complicit**

An individual is complicit in a crime if he is aware of its occurrence and has the ability to stop or report the crime, but fails to do so. As such, the individual effectively allows criminals to carry out a crime despite potentially being able to stop it from happening, either directly or by contacting the authorities. The offender is a de facto accessory to the crime, rather than an innocent bystander.

2. Corporate

In criminal law, corporate liability determines the extent to which a corporation as a legal person can be liable for the acts and omissions of the natural persons it employs. It is sometimes regarded as an aspect of criminal vicarious liability as distinct from the situation in which the wording of a statutory offence specifically attaches liability to the corporation as the principal or joint principal with a human agent.

3. **Vicarious**

This is generally applied to crimes that do not require criminal intent, e.g. those that affect the public welfare but which do not require the **imposition** of a prison term. The principle is that in such cases, the public interest is more important than private interest, and so vicarious liability is imposed to deter or to create incentives for employers to impose stricter rules and supervise more closely.

Inchoate Offense

An inchoate offense is a crime of preparing for or seeking to commit another crime. The most common example of an inchoate offense is "attempt." "Inchoate offense" has been defined as: "Conduct deemed criminal without actual harm being done, provided that the harm that would have occurred is one the law tries to prevent."

Attempt in criminal law is an offence that occurs when a person comes dangerously close to carrying out a criminal act, and intends to commit the act, but does not in fact commit it. The person may have carried out all the necessary steps (or thought they had) but still failed, or the attempt may have been abandoned or prevented at a late stage. The attempt must have gone beyond mere planning or preparation, and is distinct from other inchoate offenses such as **conspiracy** to commit a crime or **solicitation** of a crime. There are many specific crimes of attempt, such as attempted murder, which may vary by jurisdiction. Punishment is often less severe than would be the case if the attempted crime had been carried out. **Abandonment** of the attempt may constitute a not guilty defense, depending partly on the extent to which the attempt was abandoned freely and voluntarily.

Examples of inchoate offenses include conspiracy, solicitation, **facilitation**, **misprision** of **felony** (and misprision generally), organized crime, **Racketeer Influenced and Corrupt Organizations Act (RICO)**, and attempt, as well as some public health crimes.

Criminal Charge

A criminal charge is a formal **accusation** made by a governmental authority asserting that somebody has committed a crime. A charging document, which contains one or more criminal charges or counts, can take several forms, including:

- Complaint
- Information
- **Indictment**
- **Citation**
- Traffic ticket

The charging document is what generally starts a criminal case in court. But the procedure by which somebody is charged with a crime and what happens when somebody has been charged varies from country to country and even, within a country, from state to state. Before a person is proven guilty, the charge must be proven beyond a reasonable doubt.

New Words & Expressions

retribution	[ˌretrɪˈbjuːʃn]	n.	（对违法或犯罪的）惩罚；报应
deterrence	[dɪˈterəns]	n.	威慑
incapacitation	[ɪnkəpæsɪˈteɪʃən]	n.	无能力，使无能力，使无资格
rehabilitation	[ˌriːəˌbɪlɪˈteɪʃn]	n.	（罪犯的）改造，再教育；（证据法）（对证人的信誉提出异议后）证人名誉的恢复；（破产法）恢复权利
restoration	[ˌrestəˈreɪʃn]	n.	（规章制度等的）恢复；复原；（遗失等物的）归还原主；整修
actus reus		n.	[法]被告的行为，犯罪行为，犯罪意图
omission	[əˈmɪʃn]	n.	省略，删节；遗漏；疏忽；[法]不履行法律责任
mens rea		n.	[法]犯罪意图
complicit	[kəmˈplɪsɪt]	adj.	有同谋关系的，串通一气的
vicarious	[vɪˈkeərɪəs]	adj.	（想象别人苦乐情况）间接体验的；替代别人的；代理的；受委托的

imposition	[ˌɪmpəˈzɪʃn]	n.	强加；被迫接受；过分的要求；税收
inchoate offense		n.	未完成犯罪
conspiracy	[kənˈspɪrəsɪ]	n.	阴谋；反叛；共谋
solicitation	[səˌlɪsɪˈteɪʃn]	n.	诱惑；揽货；恳切地要求；游说
abandonment	[əˈbændənmənt]	n.	放弃；抛弃；遗弃；放任
facilitation	[fəˌsɪlɪˈteɪʃn]	n.	简易化，助长
misprision	[mɪsˈprɪʒən]	n.	（公职人员的）玩忽职守；渎职；包庇罪行；蔑视政府（或法庭）
felony	[ˈfelənɪ]	n.	[法] 重罪
Racketeer Influenced and Corrupt Organizations Act (RICO)			《反犯罪组织侵蚀合法组织法》
accusation	[ˌækjuˈzeɪʃn]	n.	指责，谴责；指控，控告；（被告发、控告的）罪名
indictment	[ɪnˈdaɪtmənt]	n.	诉状，起诉书；〈尤美〉刑事起诉书；控告，起诉
citation	[saɪˈteɪʃn]	n.	引用；引证；引文；表扬

Exercises

I. Choose the best answer for each of the following questions.

1. A crime may be defined as _____.

   A. a wrong committed only against persons

   B. a wrong prohibited by the common law but not statutory law

   C. a wrong prosecuted by a private attorney

   D. a wrong committed against society as a whole

2. Standard of proof in a criminal law case is _____.

   A. by a preponderance of the evidence

   B. the 50 percent rule

   C. beyond a reasonable doubt

   D. by clear and convincing evidence

3. Which of the following does NOT describe a felony?

    A. If found guilty, you are sentenced to prison for up to six months.

    B. If found guilty, you go to federal or state penitentiary.

    C. If found guilty, you may face the death penalty.

    D. If found guilty, you may face life imprisonment.

4. A wrongful mental state is known as _____.

    A. mens rea

    B. malum in se

    C. actus reus

    D. dues ex machina

5. Conspiracy

    A. At common law, an agreement between two or more persons to accomplish some criminal or unlawful purpose, or to accomplish a lawful purpose by unlawful means.

    B. Placement in a conspicuous place.

    C. The creation of counterfeit currency.

    D. A failed attempt to commit a crime.

II. Choose the proper words from the list below to fill in the blanks. Change the form of the words if necessary.

> offenders / penal / criminal / felony / property
> prosecutors / constitutional / procedures / infractions / statutes

What we call criminal law broadly refers to federal and state laws that make certain behavior illegal and punishable by imprisonment and/or fines. Our legal system is largely comprised of two different types of cases: civil and ____1____. Civil cases are disputes between people regarding the legal duties and responsibilities they owe each other. Criminal cases, meanwhile, are charges pursued by prosecutors for violations of criminal ____2____.

In the United States, British common law ruled during colonial times. Common law is a process that establishes and updates rules that govern some nations. Once America became an independent nation, it adopted the U.S. Constitution as "the supreme law of the land." The U.S. continues to employ a common law system, which works in combination with state and federal statutes. As far as criminal laws are concerned, each state has its own ____3____ code which defines what is or is not a crime, the severity of any offense and its punishment.

Criminal cases are generally categorized as felonies or misdemeanors based on their nature and the maximum imposable punishment. Each state is free to draft new criminal laws, so long as they are deemed ____4____. Thus, what is a crime in one state may not necessarily be a crime in a neighboring state.

A ____5____ involves serious misconduct that is punishable by death or by imprisonment for more than one year. Most state criminal laws subdivide felonies into different classes with varying degrees of punishment. Crimes that do not amount to felonies are typically called misdemeanors. A misdemeanor is misconduct for which the law prescribes punishment of no more than one year in prison. Lesser offenses, such as traffic and parking tickets, are often called ____6____.

Many people think that police officers (who investigate crimes) also charge ____7____. That is a common misconception. Police gather evidence and sometimes also testify in court. But ____8____ — including district attorneys, United States Attorneys and others—ultimately decide whether a suspect is prosecuted or not.

A qualified criminal defense attorney is often a crucial advocate for anyone charged with a crime. These attorneys are very familiar with local criminal ____9____ and laws — some may have even first worked as prosecutors. Most defense lawyers should be able to handle any misdemeanor or low-level crime. But not all lawyers are qualified to handle serious charges.

Some courts don't allow inexperienced attorneys to represent defendants facing capital punishment, for example. So whether you are arrested for a crime against a person (like assault and battery, rape, or murder), a crime against ____10____ (like shoplifting, burglary, or arson), or a drug crime (marijuana possession or cocaine dealing), a criminal defense lawyer can help.

UNIT 28
CRIMINAL PROCEDURE

Criminal procedure is the adjudication process of the criminal law. While criminal procedure differs dramatically by jurisdiction, the process generally begins with a formal criminal charge and results in the **conviction** or **acquittal** of the accused. Criminal procedure can be either in form of inquisitorial or adversarial criminal procedure. United States criminal procedure derives from several sources of law: the baseline protections of the United States Constitution, federal and state statutes, federal and state rules of criminal procedure (such as the Federal Rules of Criminal Procedure), and state and federal case law either interpreting the foregoing or deriving from **inherent** judicial supervisory authority.

Basic Rights

Currently, in many countries with a democratic system and the rule of law, criminal procedure puts the burden of proof on the prosecution — that is, it is up to the prosecution to prove that the defendant is guilty beyond any reasonable doubt, as opposed to having the defense prove that s/he is innocent, and any doubt is resolved in favor of the defendant. This provision, known as the presumption of innocence, is required. However, in practice it operates somewhat differently in different countries.

Similarly, all such jurisdictions allow the defendant the right to legal counsel and provide any defendant who cannot afford their own lawyer with a lawyer paid for at the public expense (which is in some countries called a "court-appointed lawyer"). The fundamental rights are as follows:

➢ Right to be informed about the crime for which the person is being arrested.

➢ Right to be presented before a judicial officer within three days of custody.

> In some countries, the accused has the right to be granted bail on application.

Charging Iinstruments

In a criminal case, the government generally brings charges in one of two ways: either by accusing a suspect directly in a "bill of information" or other similar document, or by bringing evidence before a grand jury to allow that body to determine whether the case should proceed. If the grand jury determines that there is enough evidence to justify the bringing of charges, then the defendant is indicted. In the federal system, a case must always be brought before a grand jury for **indictment** if it is punishable by death or more than one year in prison; some states, however, do not require indictment.

Petit Juries

Once charges have been brought, the case is then brought before a petit jury, (or what is commonly recognized as the normal courtroom jury of six to twelve members), or is tried by a judge alone, if the defense requests it. Any petit jury is selected from a pool by the **prosecution** and defense.

After both sides have presented their cases and made closing arguments, the judge gives the jury legal instructions; the jury then **adjourns** to **deliberate** in private. The jury generally must **unanimously** agree on a verdict of guilty or not guilty; however, the Supreme Court has upheld non unanimous jury verdicts, so long as the jury is larger than 6 people.

Verdict

1. Burden of Proof

The burden of proof is on the prosecution in a criminal trial. This means the prosecution must prove beyond a reasonable doubt that the defendant is guilty of the crime. As the defense does not have this burden, it must only prove that it is reasonable possible that the defendant did not commit the crime. The defense does not have to prove the defendant definitely did not commit the crime, only that it is possible he did not do it.

2. Deliberation

Once the prosecution and defense present their cases, the judge will give the case to the jury. First the judge will instruct the jury about any legal rules that may affect their decision. The judge then sends the jury to the jury room to deliberate about whether the defendant is guilty or innocent of the charges. During the trial the jury is not allowed to read about the case or discuss it with anyone even each other. Sometimes juries are **sequestered** or kept together away from their homes and any media coverage of the trial.

Once deliberation begins the jurors are allowed to talk to each other. They are to remain together, except overnight, until they either reach a decision or **determine** they cannot reach a decision. In the later occurrence, the jury is said to be deadlocked and is called a hung jury. If the jury decides, this is called the verdict. They inform the judge and return to the courtroom where the verdict is read. The judge may either accept the verdict or overrule it. It is rare for the verdict to be overruled. This happens when the judge thinks the verdict is unlawful. Often this is because the jury does not follow the legal instructions. It can also happen if the judge thinks the jury interpreted the evidence in a manner that was not legal. Once the verdict is determined, the trial moves to the punishment phase. This can simply be the judge issuing the punishment sentence or, in more serious cases, can involve a separate hearing.

Sentencing

If a defendant is found guilty, sentencing follows, often at a separate hearing after the prosecution, defense, and court have developed information based on which the judge will craft a sentence. The United States Sentencing Commission has **promulgated** guidance on what **restitution** and prison terms should be assessed for different crimes. In capital cases, a separate "penalty phase" occurs, in which the jury determines whether to recommend that the death penalty should be imposed. As with the determination of guilt phase, the burden is on the prosecution to prove its case, and the defendant is entitled to take the stand in his or her own defense, and may call witnesses and present evidence.

UNIT 28
CRIMINAL PROCEDURE

Appeals

After sentencing, the case enters the post conviction phase. Usually the defendant begins serving the sentence immediately after the sentence is issued. The defendant may appeal the outcome of his trial to a higher court. American appellate courts do not retry the case. These courts only examine the record of the proceedings of the lower court to determine if errors were made that require a new trial, resentencing, or a complete **dismissal** of the charges. The prosecution may not appeal after an acquittal, although it may appeal under limited circumstances before the verdict is rendered. The prosecution may also appeal the sentence itself. Increasingly, there is also a recognition that collateral consequences of criminal charges may result from the sentence that are not **explicitly** part of the sentence itself.

New Words & Expressions

conviction	[kənˈvɪkʃn]	n.	定罪；说服；确信；信念
acquittal	[əˈkwɪtl]	n.	宣告无罪；（义务、职责等的）履行；尽职；〈古〉（债务等的）清偿
inherent	[ɪnˈhɪərənt]	adj.	固有的，内在的；天生
indictment	[ɪnˈdaɪtmənt]	n.	诉状，起诉书；〈尤美〉刑事起诉书；控告，起诉
petit jury	[ˈpetiː][ˈdʒʊərɪ]	n.	小陪审团
prosecution	[ˌprɒsɪˈkjuːʃn]	n.	控告，起诉，检举；原告及其律师的总称；实施，执行，贯彻，营业；从事
adjourn	[əˈdʒɜːn]	vt.& vi.	（使）休会，（使）休庭
unanimously	[jʊˈnænɪməslɪ]	adv.	无异议地，全体一致地
deliberation	[dɪˌlɪbəˈreɪʃn]	n.	考虑，深思熟虑；评议，审议；（言语、行动等的）从容；沉着，慎重
sequester	[sɪˈkwestə(r)]	vt.	使隔绝，使隔离；〈律〉扣押
deadlock	[ˈdedlɒk]	n.	僵局；停顿，停滞；没有弹簧的锁

		vt.	停顿；相持不下
		vi.	成僵局
promulgate	['prɒmlgeɪt]	vt.	宣扬(某事物)；传播；公布；颁布(法令、新法律等)
restitution	[ˌrestɪ'tjuːʃn]	n.	归还原主；恢复原状；（尤指用钱）赔偿；补偿
dismissal	[dɪs'mɪsl]	n.	解雇，免职；撤退；解雇通知；[法]驳回，拒绝受理
explicitly	[ɪk'splɪsɪtlɪ]	adv.	明白地，明确地

Exercises

I. Choose the best answer for each of the following questions.

1. A homicide committed without malice towards the victim is known as _____.

    A. first-degree murder

    B. manslaughter

    C. a misdemeanor

    D. extortion

2. Kidnapping

    A. To tell a child to rest in the afternoon.

    B. To take and detain someone without consent or privilege.

    C. A civil action for false imprisonment.

    D. Holding a person hostage during a robbery.

3. Search warrant

    A. A warranty, as in commercial law.

    B. Document that may be issued when a defendant skips bail.

    C. Permission granted by a spouse to search a home without a warrant.

    D. Judicial order to a law enforcement officer to authorize a search and seizure of stolen property, contraband, and other evidence of criminal activity.

4. Grand jury

   A. A jury which is more intelligent than an average jury.

   B. A jury comprised of older citizens.

   C. A jury that will decide whether a criminal defendant is guilty.

   D. A jury that will decide whether there is sufficient evidence to charge a defendant with a crime.

5. Acquit

   A. Verdict of a judge or jury finding that the state has not proven guilt.

   B. Jury nullification.

   C. Voluntary termination of employment.

   D. To convict a defendant upon a showing of guilt beyond a reasonable doubt.

II. Choose the proper words from the list below to fill in the blanks. Change the form of the words if necessary.

> due process / involuntary manslaughter / presumption of innocence / misdemeanor / double jeopardy / privilege against self-incrimination / beyond a reasonable doubt / intent / infraction / probable cause

1. _____ means homicide in which there is no intention to kill or do grievous bodily harm, but that is committed with criminal negligence or during the commission of a crime not included within the felony-murder rule.

2. When a crime that is less serious than a felony and is usually punishable by fine, penalty, forfeiture, or confinement (usually for a brief term) in a place other than prison, it is referred as _____.

3. In a criminal case, the prosecutor has to prove a defendant's guilt "_____." In a civil case, the plaintiff has to show only by a "preponderance of the evidence" (more than 50 percent) that the defendant is liable for damages.

4. All criminal statutes define crimes in terms of required acts and a required stated of mind, usually described as the actor's _____. These requirements are known as the "elements" of the offense.

5. Criminal offenses are classified according to their seriousness. Today every U.S. jurisdiction retains the distinction between felony level criminal offenses and misdemeanor level offenses. However, most jurisdiction have added a third-tier of criminal offense, typically called an _____ or a petty offense.

6. There are a handful of defenses a defendant can use to get off the hook. Most often defendants try to avoid punishment by claiming they did not commit the act in question, which include the defense of the _____, reasonable doubt and the abili defense.

7. The Fifth Amendment, through the _____ Clause prohibits states from charging the same defendant with substantially the same crime on the same facts.

8. At all times during the trial, the defendant enjoys _____, i.e., a right of not having to provide testimony against themselves that could subject them to criminal prosecution. The right is guaranteed in the Fifth Amendment to the U.S. Constitution. Asserting the right is often referred to as "taking the Fifth."

9. Substantive _____ requires police to make criminal defendants aware of their rights prior to the defendant making any statements if the government intends to use those statements as evidence against the defendant.

10. _____ for search or seizure with or without search warrant involves probabilities which are not technical but factual and practical considerations of everyday life upon which reasonable and prudent men act, and its essence is reasonable ground for belief of guilt.

UNIT 29
CIVIL PROCEDURE

Civil procedure is the body of law that sets out the rules and standards that courts follow when adjudicating civil lawsuits (as opposed to procedures in criminal law matters). These rules govern how a lawsuit or case may be commenced, what kind of service of process (if any) is required, the types of **pleadings** or statements of case, motions or applications, and orders allowed in civil cases, the timing and manner of depositions and discovery or disclosure, the conduct of trials, the process for judgment, various available remedies, and how the courts and clerks must function.

Civil procedure in the United States consists of the rules of civil procedure that govern procedure in the federal courts, the 50 state court systems, and in the **territorial** courts. Like much of American law, civil procedure is not reserved to the federal government in the Constitution. As a result, each state is free to operate its own system of civil procedure independent of her sister states and the federal court system.

Personal Jurisdiction

Personal jurisdiction is a court's jurisdiction over the parties to a lawsuit, as opposed to subject-matter jurisdiction, which is jurisdiction over the law and facts involved in the suit.

1. Consent

The doctrine of consent is also extended to defendants who attend and litigate actions without challenging the court's personal jurisdiction. Consent may also derive from a pre-litigation agreement by the parties, such as a forum selection clause in a contract (not to be confused with a choice of law clause). Doctrines such as claim preclusion prevent re-litigation of failed complaints in alternative forums. Claim preclusion does not, however, prevent the refiling of a claim that was filed in a court that did not have personal jurisdiction over the defendant.

2. Power

In cases where a defendant challenges personal jurisdiction, a court may still exercise personal jurisdiction if it has independent power to do so. This power is founded in the **inherent** nature of the State: sovereignty over affairs within its territory.

3. Notice

The Fifth and Fourteenth Amendment to the United States Constitution preserve the right of the individual to due process. Due process requires that notice be given in a manner "reasonably calculated" to inform a party of the action affecting him. Originally, "Notice" (and the power of the State) was often exercised more forcefully, the defendant in a civil case sometimes being seized and brought before the court under a **writ** of **capias ad respondendum**. Notice in such a case is inferred from consent of the defendant to go with the officer. Nowadays, when exercising power over an individual without consent, notice is usually given by formal delivery of suitable papers to the defendant (service of process).

Territorial Jurisdiction

Originally, jurisdiction over parties in the United States was determined by strict interpretation of the geographic boundaries of each state's sovereign power.

1. **In personam**

In personam jurisdiction referred to jurisdiction over a particular person (or entity, such as a company). In personam jurisdiction, if held by a state court, permitted that court to rule upon any case over which it otherwise held jurisdiction.

2. **In rem**

In rem jurisdiction referred to jurisdiction over a particular piece of property, most commonly real estate or land. Certain cases, notably government suits for unpaid property taxes, proceed not against an individual but against their property directly.

3. **Quasi in rem**

Quasi in rem jurisdiction involved the **seizure** of property held by the individual against whom the suit was brought, and attachment of that property to the case in question. This form of territorial jurisdiction developed from the **rationale** of in rem jurisdiction, namely that seizure of the property was reasonably calculated to inform an individual of the proceedings against them.

Federal and State Procedural Uniformity

An express objective of the early 20th-century reformers was to use the development of new federal procedural rules to facilitate uniformity of civil procedure in the separate states. By 1959, 17 states had adopted versions of the FRCP in part or whole as their civil procedure systems. Today, 35 states have adopted versions of the **FRCP** to govern civil procedure in their state court systems, although significant modifications were necessary because the federal courts are courts of limited jurisdiction, while state courts have general jurisdiction over **innumerable** types of matters that are usually beyond the jurisdiction of federal courts (traffic, family, **probate**, and so on). In supplementing the FRCP to provide a comprehensive set of rules appropriate to state law, several states took advantage of the opportunity to impose **intrastate** uniformity of civil procedure, thereby cutting down on the ability of trial court judges in rural areas to trip up big city lawyers with obscure local rules and forms, and in turn improving the portability of legal services. Even states that declined to adopt the FRCP, like California, also joined the movement towards intrastate uniformity of civil procedure.

Notable Features

Generally, American civil procedure has several notable features, including extensive pretrial discovery, heavy reliance on live testimony obtained at deposition or elicited in front of a jury, and aggressive pretrial "law and motion" practice designed to result in a pretrial disposition (that is, summary judgment) or a settlement. U.S. courts pioneered the concept of the opt-out class action, by which the burden falls on class members to notify the court that they do not wish to be bound by the judgment, as opposed to opt-in class actions, where class members must join into the class. Another unique feature is the so-called American Rule under which parties generally bear their own attorneys' fees (as opposed to the English Rule of "loser pays"), though American legislators and courts have carved out numerous exceptions.

Differences between Civil and Criminal Procedure

In jurisdictions based on English common-law systems, the party bringing a criminal charge (in most cases, the state) is called the "**prosecution**", but the party bringing most forms of civil action is the "plaintiff" or "claimant." In both kinds of action the other party is known as the "defendant." A criminal case against a person called Ms. Sanchez would be described as *"The People v. (='versus', 'against' or 'and') Sanchez," "The State (or Commonwealth) v. Sanchez"* or *"[The name of the State] v. Sanchez"* in the United States and *"R. (Regina, that is, the Queen) v. Sanchez"* in England and Wales. But a civil action between Ms. Sanchez and a Mr. Smith would be *"Sanchez v. Smith"* if it were started by Sanchez, and *"Smith v. Sanchez"* if it were started by Mr. Smith (though the order of parties' names can change if the case is appealed).

The standards of proof are higher in a criminal case than in a civil one, since the state does not wish to risk punishing an innocent person. In English law the prosecution must prove the guilt of a criminal "beyond reasonable doubt"; but the plaintiff in a civil action is required to prove his case "on the balance of probabilities." Thus, in a criminal case a crime cannot be proven if the person or persons judging it doubt the guilt of the suspect and have a reason (not just a feeling or intuition) for this doubt. But in a civil case, the court will weigh all the evidence and decide what is most probable.

New Words & Expressions

pleading	['pli:dɪŋ]	*n.*	恳求，请求；辩论，辩护；[法]诉状；诉讼程序
		adj.	恳求的，请求的
		v.	恳求，请求（plead 的现在分词）；抗辩，答辩；恳求，请求
territorial	[ˌterəˈtɔ:rɪəl]	*adj.*	领土的；区域的；土地的；地方的

UNIT 29
CIVIL PROCEDURE

		n.	地方自卫队士兵
pre-litigation	[ˌprɪlaɪˈbeɪʃən]	n.	诉前
re-litigation	[ˌlɪtɪˈgeɪʃn]	n.	再诉讼
inherent	[ɪnˈhɪərənt]	adj.	固有的，内在的；天生
writ	[rɪt]	n.	［法］令状；文书；法院命令
capias ad respondendum			［法］拘提轻罪案被告以便讯问令
in personam			＜拉＞对某人不利，将某人起诉
in rem			＜拉＞对物（指判决的对象是物或财产）诉讼地（的）；对物权
quasi in rem		adj.	［法］通过对财产或不动产的司法权，所产生的对人的司法权
seizure	[ˈsiːʒə(r)]	n.	没收；夺取；捕捉；突然发作
rationale	[ˌræʃəˈnɑːl]	n.	理论的说明；基本原理，基础理论；根据
FRCP			Federal Rules of Civil Procedure
innumerable	[ɪˈnjuːmərəbl]	adj.	无数的，数不清的；指不胜屈；不可胜数；无可胜数
probate	[ˈprəʊbeɪt]	n.	遗嘱检验，经检验的遗嘱文本
		vt.	［法］遗嘱认证；处以缓刑；加以监护；在遗嘱认证法庭证明……精神失常
		adj.	［法］遗嘱认证的
intrastate	[ˌɪntrəˈsteɪt]	adj.	州内的（尤指美国的州内）
opt-out	[ɒpt aʊt]	n.	自愿退出；不参加
prosecution	[ˌprɒsɪˈkjuːʃn]	n.	控告，起诉，检举；原告及其律师的总称

Exercises

I. Choose the best answer for each of the following questions.

1. Class action refers to _____.

    A. a revolt by students

B. a lawsuit brought on behalf of a single individual

C. a lawsuit brought on behalf of a corporation

D. a lawsuit brought by or on behalf of a group

2. Directed verdict means _____.

   A. a ruling by the judge upon finding that the evidence so favors one party that it is not even necessary for the jury to make a decision

   B. a judgment against the directors of a corporation

   C. a jury verdict after trial

   D. a term of art for the type of evidence that is often excluded, unless it falls within an accepted category

3. Cross-examination refers to _____.

   A. inspection liability law for persons

   B. direct examination of a witness

   C. questioning of an adverse witness

   D. questioning of a party's own witness

4. Deposition refers to _____.

   A. a tool of discovery used before trial

   B. statements made by a witness on the witness stand during trial (also known as "trial testimony")

   C. the position a defendant is placed in while waiting for a trial

   D. the court's resolution of a case

5. Judicial Notice means _____.

   A. spotting of a judge who is standing in an elevator or walking on the street

   B. the spotting by a judge of a lawyer who is unlawfully speaking to a juror (i.e., a member of the jury) during a break in the court proceedings

   C. a procedure that allows a court to admit certain facts into evidence without the usual requirements of proof when those facts are either generally known or because they are readily verifiable by reliable sources

   D. a procedure where judges with special expertise in a technical area can

UNIT 29
CIVIL PROCEDURE

substitute their own knowledge for the testimony of an expert witness.

II. **Choose the proper words from the list below to fill in the blanks. Change the form of the words if necessary.**

> removal / in personam / state statues / venue / in rem
> consent / good faith / quasi in rem / multiple party / proceedings

1. Lawyers use the Federal Rules of Civil Procedure for _____ in the federal courts.
2. Limitations on a court's personal jurisdiction arise from two sources: the United States Constitution and _____.
3. _____ jurisdiction exists when the forum has power over the person of a particular defendant.
4. _____ jurisdiction exists when the court has power to adjudicate the rights of all persons in the world with respect to a particular item of property.
5. One type of _____ jurisdiction exists when the court has power to determine whether particular individual own specific property within the court's control.
6. _____ is the designation of the proper district in which to bring an action.
7. A defendant may _____ to jurisdiction by a voluntary appearance, i.e., by contesting the case without challenging personal jurisdiction.
8. _____ questions concern whether various types of joinder are permitted under federal law and, if so, whether there is a jurisdictional basis for a particular attempted joinder.
9. _____ means that there must be a legally tenable possibility that recovery will exceed the jurisdictional amount.
10. _____ jurisdiction allows defendants to remove an action brought in a state court to a federal court if the federal court would have had original jurisdiction over the action.

163

UNIT 30
BUSINESS LAW

Business law is the body of law that applies to the rights, relations, and conduct of persons and businesses engaged in commerce, merchandising, trade, and sales. It is often considered to be a branch of civil law and deals with issues of both private law and public law. In the United States, commercial law is the province of both the United States Congress, under its power to regulate interstate commerce, and the states, under their police power. Efforts have been made to create a unified body of commercial law in the United States; the most successful of these attempts has resulted in the general adoption of the Uniform Commercial Code, which has been adopted in all 50 states (with some modification by state legislatures), the District of Columbia, and the U.S. territories.

Types of Business Entity

A business entity is an entity that is formed and administered as per commercial law in order to engage in business activities, **charitable** work, or other activities allowable. Most often, business entities are formed to sell a product or a service. There are many types of business entities defined in the legal systems of various countries. These include corporations, cooperatives, partnerships, sole traders, limited liability company and other specifically permitted and labelled types of entities. The specific rules vary by country and by state or province. Some of these types are listed below, by country.

However, the regulations governing particular types of entity, even those described as roughly equivalent, differ from jurisdiction to jurisdiction. When creating or **restructuring** a business, the legal responsibilities will depend on the type of business **entity** chosen.

Corporate Law

Corporate law (also "company" or "corporations" law) is the study of how shareholders, directors, employees, creditors, and other stakeholders such as consumers, the community and the environment interact with one another. Corporate law is a part of a broader company's law (or law of business associations). Other types of business associations can include partnerships (in the U.K. governed by the Partnership Act 1890), or trusts (like a pension fund), or companies limited by guarantee (like some community organizations or charities). Under corporate law, corporations of all sizes have separate legal personality, with limited or unlimited liability for its shareholders. Shareholders control the company through a board of directors which, in turn, typically delegates control of the corporation's day-to-day operations to a full-time executive. Corporate law deals with firms that are incorporated or registered under the corporate or company law of a sovereign state or their subnational states. The four defining characteristics of the modern corporation are:

➢ Separate legal personality of the corporation (access to tort and contract law in a manner similar to a person);

➢ Limited liability of the shareholders (a shareholder's personal liability is limited to the value of their shares in the corporation);

➢ Shares (if the corporation is a public company, the shares are traded on a stock exchange);

➢ Delegated management; the board of directors' delegates day-to-day management of the company to executives.

Security (Finance)

A security is a tradable financial asset. The term commonly refers to any form of financial instrument, but its legal definition varies by jurisdiction. In some jurisdictions the term specifically excludes financial instruments other than equities and fixed income instruments. In some jurisdictions it includes some instruments that are close to equities and fixed income, e.g. equity **warrants**. In some countries and/or languages the term "security" is commonly used in day-to-day **parlance** to mean any form of financial instrument, even though the underlying legal and regulatory regime may not have such a broad definition.

In the U.S.A., a security is a tradable financial asset of any kind. Securities are broadly categorized into:

➤ Debt securities (e.g. banknotes, bonds and **debentures**).

➤ Equity securities (e.g. common stocks).

➤ Derivatives (e.g. forwards, futures, options and **swaps**).

The company or other entity issuing the security is called the issuer. A country's regulatory structure determines what qualifies as a security. For example, private investment pools may have some features of securities, but they may not be registered or regulated as such if they meet various restrictions.

Securities may be represented by a certificate or, more typically, "non-certificated", that is in electronic (**dematerialized**) or "book entry" only form. Certificates may be bearer, meaning they entitle the holder to rights under the security merely by holding the security, or registered, meaning they entitle the holder to rights only if he or she appears on a security register maintained by the issuer or an intermediary. They include shares of corporate stock or mutual funds, bonds issued by corporations or governmental agencies, stock options or other options, limited partnership units, and various other formal investment instruments that are negotiable and **fungible**.

Commercial Paper

Commercial paper, in the global financial market, is an unsecured **promissory** note with a fixed **maturity** of no more than 270 days.

Commercial paper is a money-market security issued (sold) by large corporations to obtain funds to meet short-term debt obligations (for example, **payroll**), and is backed only by an issuing bank or company promise to pay the face amount on the maturity date specified on the note. Since it is not backed by **collateral**, only firms with excellent credit ratings from a recognized credit rating agency will be able to sell their commercial paper at a reasonable price. Commercial paper is usually sold at a discount from face value, and generally carries lower interest repayment rates than bonds due to the shorter maturities of commercial paper. Typically, the longer the maturity on a note, the higher the interest rate the issuing institution pays. Interest rates fluctuate with market conditions, but are typically lower than banks' rates.

Commercial paper — though a short-term obligation — is issued as part of a continuous rolling program, which is either a number of years long (as in Europe), or open-ended (as in the U.S.).

New Words & Expressions

charitable	[ˈtʃærətəbl]	adj.	仁慈的,慈善的;宽恕的,宽厚的;慷慨的
restructure	[ˌriːˈstrʌktʃə(r)]	v.	重建;调整;重组
equities	[ˈekwɪtɪz]	n.	股票;普通股
warrant	[ˈwɒrənt]	n.	授权证;许可证;正当理由;依据
		vt.	保证,担保;授权,批准;辩解
parlance	[ˈpɑːləns]	n.	腔调,说法,用语
debenture	[dɪˈbentʃə(r)]	n.	公司债券
derivative	[dɪˈrɪvətɪv]	n.	[数]导数,微商;[化]衍生物,派生物;[语]派生词
		adj.	衍生的;导出的;拷贝的
swap	[swɒp]	n.	交换;交换物,被调换者
		vi.	交换(工作)
		vt.	用……替换,把……换成,调换(过来)
dematerialized	[diːməˈtɪərɪəlaɪzd]	n.	非物质化
fungible	[ˈfʌndʒɪbl]	adj.	可互换的,代替的
		n.	代替物
promissory	[ˈprɒmɪsərɪ]	adj.	应允的,承诺的,约定的

maturity	[mə'tʃʊərətɪ]	n.	成熟；完备；（票据等的）到期
payroll	['peɪrəʊl]	n.	工资名单；工资总支出，工薪总额
collateral	[kə'lætərəl]	n.	担保物；旁系亲属
		adj.	并行的；附属的；旁系的

Exercises

I. Choose the best answer for each of the following questions.

1. In disputes over whether a partnership exists, which of the following is NOT considered to be an essential element?

    A. An equal right in the management of the business.

    B. The sharing of profits or losses.

    C. The consultation on business strategy.

    D. Joint ownership in the business.

2. How were partnerships treated under the common law?

    A. As separate legal entities.   B. As aggregates of members.

    C. As corporations.   D. As sole proprietorships.

3. When a group of members join to form a LLC, the name of their organization _____.

    A. must convey the purpose of their organization

    B. must be registered with the SEC

    C. must include the words "limited liability corporation" or the letters "LLC"

    D. must be approved by a vote of the state legislature

4. A corporation is a legal entity _____.

    A. created by the local government

    B. created and recognized by an entrepreneurial agency

    C. managed internally by the federal government

    D. created and recognized by state law in most cases

UNIT 30
BUSINESS LAW

5. The responsibility for the overall management of a corporation belongs to _____.

    A. the chief financial officer   B. the employees

    C. the board of directors   D. the shareholders

II. Choose the proper words from the list below to fill in the blanks. Change the form of the words if possible.

> commercial paper / issuer / entities / fluctuate / shareholders
>
> maturity / security / restructure / promissory / corporate law

1. There are many types of business _____ defined in the legal systems of various countries.

2. When creating or _____ a business, the legal responsibilities will depend on the type of business entity chosen.

3. _____ control the company through a board of directors which, in turn, typically delegates control of the corporation's day-to-day operations to a full-time executive.

4. A _____ is a tradable financial asset.

5. The company or other entity issuing the security is called the _____.

6. _____ deals with firms that are incorporated or registered under the corporate or company law of a sovereign state or their subnational states.

7. _____ is usually sold at a discount from face value, and generally carries lower interest repayment rates than bonds due to the shorter maturities of _____.

8. Commercial paper is backed only by an issuing bank or company promise to pay the face amount on the _____ date specified on the note.

9. Typically, the longer the _____ on a note, the higher the interest rate the issuing institution pays.

10. Interest rates _____ with market conditions, but are typically lower than banks' rates.

KEY TO THE EXERCISES

UNIT 1   REPORTING A CRIME

I. Translate the following dialogue.

A: I want to report a crime, sir.

B: What's happened ?

A: I was robbed of my handbag.

B: When did it happen?

A: Just now, about 15 minutes ago.

B: Where did it happen? And how?

A: I went to the supermarket to do some shopping. Shortly after I came out, a man from behind took away my handbag and ran. I tried to catch up with him but he disappeared in a while.

B: What does your handbag look like?

A: It is pink, a Fortune Duck. It is still quite new. A key ring is fastened to the belt.

B: What are the things in the bag?

A: There are a wallet, a cellular phone and a black umbrella. And in the wallet are 300 yuan and I.D. card and an Employee's card.

B: What does the man look like? Could you please describe him?

A: He's not tall, quite thin, with a moustache on his face.

B: What kind of clothes was he wearing? What colour?

A: White shirt with long-sleeves, dark blue jeans. I can't say for sure.

B: Is this all? Do you want to add something else?

A: No, this is all that I can remember.

B: Ok, please leave your name, address and means of contact. We will start the investigation as soon as possible. Once there is new information we will contact you.

UNIT 2   CONSULTING A LAWYER

I. Change the sentences to a more polite form.

1. Could you be sure to arrive on time for your scheduled appointment?
2. Can you tell me if there's any possibility of winning the case?
3. Will you please tell me what I should do if I just cannot afford a quality lawyer?
4. I wonder if you could recommend a good lawyer to me.
5. Would you please tell me when the court will hear this case.

UNIT 3   ARBITRATION

I. Interpret the following dialogue.

A: 我和彼得做生意有了些纠纷，我不知该怎样解决才好？怀特先生，你说呢？

B: 你想告他吗？

A: 打官司通常耗时又耗力。我不想拖得太久，况且彼得是我的老客户了，我不想伤了和气。有没有其他的解决办法？

B: 有的。不知你听说过 ADR 没有？

A: 听说过。好像是指那些不同于传统的法院诉讼程序的其他解决纠纷的方式。

B: 是的。它有许多形式，包括仲裁、调解、谈判等等。这些你都可以考虑。

A: 哪一种方式更好呢？

B: 每种方式都有利有弊。这要根据具体情况来做出选择。通常，调节主要用于劳资纠纷。它促使双方达成协议并提出解决纠纷的建议，但这些建议对双方都没有约束力。

UNIT 4　PLEA BARGAINING

I. Choose the proper words from the list below to fill in the blanks. Change the form of the words if necessary.

1. criminal
2. prosecutor
3. concession
4. guilty
5. dismissal
6. original
7. lenient
8. lengthy
9. conviction
10. serious

UNIT 5　CHARACTERISTICS OF LEGAL ENGLISH

I. Judge whether the statements below are true (T) or false (F).

1. F　　2. F　　3. T　　4. F　　5. F
6. T　　7. F　　8. T　　9. F　　10. F

II. Use your dictionary and find out the meaning of the following words and expressions in legal context. Discuss with your classmates the meaning differences between legal context and everyday English.

1. accord

    释义：accord 在普通英语中的含义是符合，一致的意思，在法律英语中则表示和解或和解协议，指债务人和一个债权人达成的、以偿还部分债务免除全部债务责任的协议。如 reach an accord 达成和解协议，accord and satisfaction 和解与清偿等。

2. acquire

    释义：acquire 在普通英语中的含义是获得，获取的意思，而且通常指通过后天的努力获得。在法律英语中通常指对公司的购买，收购。

3. composition

   释义：composition 在普通英语中的常见意思为作文，结构的意思，在法律英语中的意思为和解协议，指债务人与全部或至少相当一部分债权人达成的此类协议。

4. discharge

   释义：1）履行，侧重于对具体义务的履行，相当于 fulfill；

   2）免除，即免除他人的义务或债务。例如，His liability to pay the loan to the bank was discharged due to his bankruptcy。他对银行的借款偿还义务因其破产而免除。

5. enter into

   释义：enter into 仅仅用在法律英语中，且通常表示合同的订立。

6. grace

   释义：（还款）宽限期，如 day of grace，grace period 宽限期等。

7. infant

   释义：infant 的一般含义是婴儿，但在法律英语中表示未成年人。

8. principal

   释义：principal 在法律英语中指本人，贷款中的本金。如 principal and agent 本人和代理，principal and interest 本金和利息。

9. secure

   释义：secure 在法律英语中的意思是担保，而不是普通英语中的获取或形容词安全的，如 secured bond 担保债券，secured note 有担保的本票。

10. without prejudice to

    释义：without prejudice to 是法律英语中常见的一个词组，意思是不损害。

UNIT 6　DOCTRINE OF STARE DECISIS

I. Choose the best answer for each of the following questions.

1. B　　2. C　　3. A

II. Choose the proper words from the list below to fill in the blanks. Change the form the words if necessary.

1. Latin   2. disregard   3. prior   4. essence   5. appellate
6. hears   7. decisions   8. trial   9. future   10. identical

UNIT 7   COURT ETIQUETTE AND ATTIRE

I. Judge whether the statements below are true (T) or false (F).

1. F   2. F   3. F   4. T   5. T
6. F   7. F   8. T   9. F   10. T

II. Choose the proper words from the list below to fill in the blanks. Change the form of the words if necessary.

1. attire   2. contempt   3. affect   4. representative   5. process
6. prepared   7. business   8. disruptive   9. permission   10. formal

UNIT 8   LEGAL ETHICS

I. Judge whether the statements below are true (T) or false (F).

1. T   2. F   3. F   4. F   5. T
6. F   7. F   8. T   9. F   10. T

II. Translate the following paragraph about legal ethics into Chinese.

　　复杂的法律实践中往往间杂着许多道德问题。法律伦理规定了法律从业者的职业行为准则。作为法律从业者，他们必须遵守基本的法律职业道德规范，如果一旦涉及违反职业道德，就有可能会因此被吊销从业执照。随着新的法律问题的不断地出现，许多法学院和律师协会定期建议修改职业道德准则，以帮助法律执业人员了解新的职业道德问题，从而确保他们的利益。

KEY TO THE EXERCISES

UNIT 9   CHIEF JUSTICE IN THE UNITED STATES

I. Judge whether the statements below are true (T) or false (F).

1. T   2. F   3. F   4. F   5. F
6. F   7. T   8. F   9. F   10. T

II. Translate the following duties of the Chief Justice in the U.S. Supreme court into Chinese.

1. 在（最高法院的）大法官们慎重考虑之后，首席大法官第一个进入法庭并首先投票。首席大法官的投票和其他（8位）大法官的选票分量相当。
2. 在最高法院案件的判决中，如果首席大法官的投票与绝大多数投票意见一致时，他或她可能会选择写法庭意见，或将任务分配给其他大法官中的一位。
3. 首席大法官主持弹劾美国总统。
4. 在美国总统就职典礼上，首席大法官主持总统的履职宣誓，这纯粹是一个传统职责。
5. 首席大法官每年向国会递交一份关于联邦法庭体系状况的报告。

UNIT 10   LAWYERS

I. Judge whether the statements below are true (T) or false (F).

1. F   2. T   3. F   4. F   5. T
6. F   7. T   8. T   9. F   10. F

II. Choose appropriate words to finish the passage below about the lawyers' responsibilities. Change the form of the words if necessary.

1. attorney   2. evidence   3. advisors   4. counseling
5. property   6. transactions   7. conform   8. enforcement
9. judicial   10. conferring

UNIT 11 COMMON LAW & CIVIL LAW SYSTEM

I. Complete the following chart about the differences between the common law and civil law with the information you've got from the passage.

	common law	civil law
History	It have evolved primarily in <u>England</u> and its former <u>colonies</u>, including Australia, Canada, England, India and the United States.	It developed in <u>continental Europe</u> at the same time and was applied in the colonies of <u>European imperial powers</u> such as Spain and Portugal.
Legal system	Legal system is largely based on <u>precedents</u>, which is <u>the judicial decisions</u> that have already been made in similar cases.	Legal system originating in Europe whose primary source of law is <u>legal codes</u> that specify all matters capable of being brought before a court
Roles of judges	Judges make laws. They <u>moderate</u> between lawyers and determines the <u>appropriate sentence</u> based on the jury's verdict.	The judge takes on an <u>inquisitional</u> role to establish <u>the facts of the case</u> by asking the parties questions and to apply the provisions of <u>the applicable code</u>. Its decisions are not the major source of civil law.
Types of argument in the court	<u>Adversarial</u>. A contest between two opposing parties before a judge.	Inquisitorial. Judges, not lawyers, ask questions and demand evidence.
Jury	A jury of <u>ordinary people without legal training</u> decides on <u>the facts of the case</u>.	

II. Choose the best answer for each of the following questions.

1. B   2. A   3. D   4. C   5. A   6. C   7. A   8. B

UNIT 12   JURY TRIAL

I. Choose the best answer for each of the following questions.

1. B   2. D   3. A   4. A   5. D

II. Choose the proper words from the list below to fill in the blanks. Change the form of the words if necessary.

1. institution   2. represent   3. observe   4. instructions   5. involved
6. verdict   7. witnesses   8. accused   9. innocent   10. guarantee

UNIT 13   COURT SYSTEM IN THE UNITED STATES

I. Choose the proper words from the list below to fill in the blanks. Change the form of the words if necessary.

1. jurisdiction   2. file   3. review   4. appeal   5. decision
6. authorizing   7. judicial   8. discretion   9. render   10. regulate

II. Translate the following phrases into English.

1. lower court   2. the Supreme Court   3. appellate court/ court of appeal
4. district court   5. circuit court   6. trial court
7. intermediate court   8. original jurisdiction
9. civil case   10. criminal case

III. Translate the following passage into Chinese.

　　法院解释法律。它们也处理个人与政府之间的纠纷。不同级别的法院处理不同种类的案子。联邦法院处理与宪法和议会所制定的法律有关的案子,它们也处理州与州之间,或几个州之间的问题。最高法院是司法部门中最高级别的法院。最高法院的法官被称为大法官。最高法院的负责人是首席大法官。宪法的制定者认为如果法官由公民选举,选举出来的法官可能会偏袒这部分的公民。出于这个考虑,法官不是由选举产生的,他们是被任命的。所有联邦法院的法官都是由总统任命的。然而,所有总统的任命必须得到参议院的批准。法官的任期是终身制的。像总统一样,他们也会受到弹劾,接受审判,以及被要求离职。

UNIT 14 SOURCES OF LAW IN THE UNITED STATES

I. Match each legal term with its proper definition.

1. c 2. e 3. g 4. j 5. i 6. k 7. d 8. a 9. f 10. b 11. H

II. Complete the following figure with the information from the passage to show the relationships among the branches of government and types of legal rules they create.

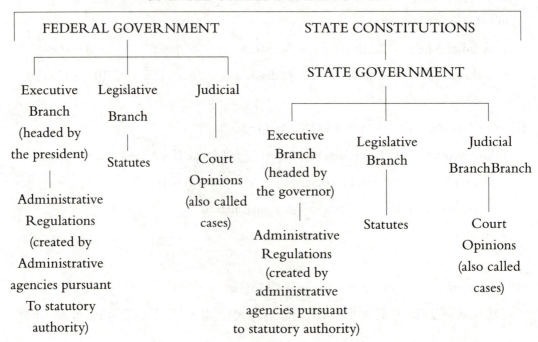

III. Judge whether the statements below are true (T) or false (F).

1. F 2. T 3. F 4. F 5. T

UNIT 15   SEVEN PRINCIPLES IN THE U.S. JUDICIAL SYSTEM

I. Match each word with its proper definition.

1. j   2. h   3. e   4. i   5. a
6. g   7. b   8. f   9. c   10. d

II. Translate the following sentences into Chinese.

1. 三权分立这项原则要求国家的三大权力机关——立法、行政和司法——中的各方都有独立不同的责任和职能。
2. 法院的命令和判决是法官根据法律并在适用已被公认和既定的法律原则、规则的基础上做出的,法院的命令和判决既不是法官根据诉讼当事人的地位,也不是接受国家机关以内或以外某个人或机构的要求和影响做出的。
3. 通过该程序,律师代表其诉讼委托人——诉讼当事人——想方设法呈示证据,摆出法律理由从而把一个案件的所有事实和观点提供给法官或陪审团,以便他们做出公正的判决。
4. 正当程序的要求为因国家机关的行为、法律的实施或其他国家机关的决定而受到伤害或蒙受损失的个人保证其有权参加法院的听审,以便陈述冤屈以及有关的意见和理由,并请求纠正和补偿。

UNIT 16   LEGAL PROFESSIONALS IN THE UNITED STATES

I. Choose the best answer to complete the following statements.

1. D   2. A   3. C   4. B   5. B

II. Choose the proper words from the list below to fill in the blanks. Change the form of the words if necessary.

1. appointed   2. approved   3. impeachment   4. nomination   5. practicing
6. general   7. evidence   8. defender   9. licensed   10. accredited

UNIT 17   LEGAL AID IN THE UNITED STATES

I. Choose the best answer for each of the following questions.

1. C   2. D   3. B   4. A   5. C   6. A

II. Match each legal term with its proper definition.

1. e   2. g   3. b   4. a   5. i   6. f   7. c   8. j   9. h   10. d

UNIT 18   LEGAL EDUCATION IN THE UNITED STATES

I. Choose the best answer for each of the following questions.

1. C   2. A   3. C   4. D   5. A   6. B

II. Choose the proper words from the list below to fill in the blanks. Change the form of the words if necessary.

1. share   2. particular   3. branch   4. fundamentally   5. acquisition
6. legal   7. analytical   8. reflects 9. graduates   10. encounter
11. professional

UNIT 19   WORLD TRADE ORGANIZATION (I)

I. Choose the best answer for each of the following questions.

1. B   2. D   3. B   4. A   5. B   6. C   7. D

KEY TO THE EXERCISES

II. Write the full name of the following abbreviations and then translate them into Chinese.

1. the World Trade Organization 世贸组织
2. the General Agreement on Tariffs and Trade 关贸总协定
3. the General Agreement on Trade in Services 服务业贸易总协定
4. the Agreement on Trade-Related Aspects of Intellectual Property Rights 与贸易有关的知识产权协定
5. the Trade Related Investment Measures 与贸易有关的投资措施

III. Translate the following paragraph into Chinese.

世界贸易组织总部设在瑞士日内瓦，它是一个政府间组织，负责管理国际贸易。世贸组织于 1995 年 1 月 1 日根据《马拉喀什协议》正式开始运作，该《协议》由 123 个国家签署于 1994 年 4 月 15 日，取代了于 1948 年开始的关税和贸易总协定。世贸组织监管成员国之间的贸易，为其贸易协议的谈判提供了一个框架，并且提供了争端解决程序，旨在强制参与国遵守由成员国政府代表签署并由他们的议会批准的世贸组织协议。

UNIT 20　WORLD TRADE ORGANIZATION (II)

I. Choose the proper words from the list below to fill in the blanks. Change the form of the words if necessary.

1. dispute　　2. binding　　3. priority　　4. complainant　　5. implement
6. mediated　　7. violate　　8. compulsory　　9. invoke　　10. adjudicate

II. Check (√) the functions of WTO.

3,　　4,　　6,　　7,

III. Judge whether the statements below are true (T) or false (F).

1. F 2. F 3.T 4.T 5.F 6.F 7.T 8. T

UNIT 21 CONSTITUTIONAL LAW

I. Choose the best answer for each of the following questions.

1. B 2. B 3.B 4.D 5. D

II. Matching each legal term with proper definition.

1. b 2. j 3. a 4. c 5. g
6. e 7. f 8. d 9. h 10.i

UNIT 22 CONTRACTS

I. Choose the proper explanation to each of the following legal terms.

1. D 2. C 3.B 4.D 5. B

II. Choose the proper words from the list below to fill in the blanks. Change the form of the words if necessary.

1. agreement   2. mutual   3. damages   4. enforce
5. remedy   6. binding   7. benefit   8. adequate
9. assurance   10. consideration

UNIT 23 TORTS

I. Choose the proper explanation to each of the follawing legal terms.

1. C 2. B 3. D 4. C 5. D

KEY TO THE EXERCISES

II. Choose the proper words from the list below to fill in the blanks. Change the form of the words if necessary.

1. civil   2. property   3. plaintiff   4. litigation   5. compensate
6. punitive   7. defendants   8. malicious   9. gravity   10. liability

UNIT 24   PROPERTY LAW

I. Choose the proper words from the list below to fill in the blanks. Change the form of the words if necessary.

1. property   2. infringement   3. intellectual property rights
4. concurrent estate   5. leasehold   6. Lien
7. easement   8. adverse possession   9. Bailment   10. nuisances

II. Choose the proper words from the list below to fill in the blanks. Change the form of the words if necessary.

1. obligations   2. voluntarily   3. contract   4. liable   5. consideration
6. parties   7. promises   8. enforce   9. offering   10. agreement

UNIT 25   EVIDENCE LAW

I. Choose the proper words from the list below to fill in the blanks. Change the form of the words if necessary.

1. demonstrative   2. admissibility   3. exclusionary   4. relevant
5. competent   6. existence   7. defendant   8. duress   9. foundation
10. authentication

II. Translate the following sentences into Chinese.

1. 证据是从中可以推导出合理结论的任何陈述或者实物。

2. 刑事审判中的证据涉及犯罪的目的、动机、方法和机会。
3. 间接证据包括通过证人收集的信息以及指证某一个人为犯罪实施者的书证（文书）。
4. 司法鉴定人员的工作就是要检验实物证据，使用科学方法再现构成犯罪的事实。
5. 允许专家证人根据事实进行法官或者陪审团不能进行的推理。

UNIT 26　INTELLECTUAL PROPERTY LAW

I. Judge whether the statements below are true (T) or false (F).

1. T　　2. F　　3. F　　4. F　　5. T

II. Translate the following paragraph into Chinese.

专利权是由联邦政府授予的对一项发明享有的使用、制造和销售的专有权，其期限为17年，如果专利权是授予一项外观设计的，专有使用权的期限则不得超过14年。专利法旨在促进艺术和科学的发展，奖励发明人。如果发明人对其发明没有一定期限的专有使用权，发明人可能不会积极将其发明推向公众。因此，为了鼓励发明人向公众展示其专利，专利法授予专利权人一定期限制造、使用和买卖其发明的专有权，他们还可以利用政府授予的专利权进行盈利，当然这一点并不是专利法的主要目的。只有某产品在外国也被授予专利权，发明者才可以获得专利的国际保护。许多国家都有保护专利权人的法律，保护成员国专利权的国际条约也已签署。

UNIT 27　CRIMINAL LAW

I. Choose the best answer for each of the following questions.

1. D　　2. C　　3. A　　4. A　　5. A

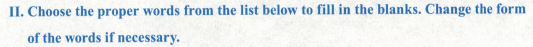

II. Choose the proper words from the list below to fill in the blanks. Change the form of the words if necessary.

1. criminal
2. statutes
3. penal
4. constitutional
5. felony
6. infractions
7. offenders
8. prosecutors
9. procedures
10. property

UNIT 28   CRIMINAL PROCEDURE

I. Choose the best answer for each of the following questions.

1. B   2. B   3. D   4. D   5. A

II. Choose the proper words from the list below to fill in the blanks. Change the form of the words if necessary.

1. involuntary manslaughter
2. misdemeanor
3. beyond a reasonable doubt
4. intent
5. infraction
6. due process
7. double jeopardy
8. privilege against self-incrimination
9. presumption of innocence
10. Probable cause

UNIT 29   CIVIL PROCEDURE

I. Choose the best answer for each of the following questions.

1. D   2. A   3. C   4. A   5. C

II. Choose the proper words from the list below to fill in the blanks. Change the form of the words if necessary.

1. proceedings
2. state statues
3. In personam
4. In rem
5. quasi in rem
6. Venue
7. consent
8. Multiple party

9. Good faith   10. Removal

UNIT 30 BUSINESS LAW

I. Choose the best answer for each of the following questions.

1. C   2. B   3. C   4. D   5. C

II. Choose the proper words from the list below to fill in the blanks. Change the form of the words if necessary.

1. entities   2. restructure   3. Hareholders   4. security

5. issuer   6. Corporate law   7. Commercial paper   8. promissory

9. maturity   10. fluctuate

APPENDIX A
HOW TO BRIEF CASES AND ANALYZE CASE PROBLEMS

How to Brief Cases

To fully understand the law with respect to business, you need to be able to read and understand court decisions. To make this task easier, you can use a method of case analysis that is called briefing. There is a fairly standard procedure that you can follow when you "brief" any court case. You must first read the case opinion carefully. When you feel you understand the case, you can prepare a brief of it.

Although the format of the brief may vary, typically it will present the essentials of the case under headings such as those listed below.

1 Citation. Give the full citation for the case, including the name of the case, the date it was decided, and the court that decided it.

2 Facts. Briefly indicate (a) the reasons for the lawsuit; (b) the identity and arguments of the plaintiff(s) and defendant(s), respectively; and (c) the lower court's decision—if appropriate.

3 Issue. Concisely phrase, in the form of a question, the essential issue before the court. (If more than one issue is involved, you may have two—or even more—questions here.)

4 Decision. Indicate here—with a "yes" or "no," if possible—the court's answer to the question (or questions) in the Issue section above.

5 Reason. Summarize as briefly as possible the reasons given by the court for its decision (or decisions) and the case or statutory law relied on by the court in arriving at its decision.

An Example of a Brief Sample Court Case

As an example of the format used in briefing cases, we present here a briefed version of the sample court case that was presented in the following parts.

BERGER v. CITY OF SEATTLE
United States Court of Appeals,
Ninth Circuit, 2008.
512 F.3d 582.

FACTS The Seattle Center is an entertainment "zone" in downtown Seattle, Washington, that attracts nearly ten million tourists each year. The center encompasses theaters, arenas, museums, exhibition halls, conference rooms, outdoor stadiums, and restaurants, and features street performers. Under the authority of the city, the center's director issued rules in 2002 to address safety concerns and other matters. Among other things, street performers were required to obtain permits and wear badges. After members of the public filed numerous complaints of threatening behavior by street performer and balloon artist Michael Berger, Seattle Center staff cited Berger for several rules violations. He filed a suit in a federal district court against the city and others, alleging, in part, that the rules violated his free speech rights under the First Amendment to the U.S. Constitution. The court issued a judgment in the plaintiff's favor. The city appealed to the U.S. Court of Appeals for the Ninth Circuit.

ISSUE Did the rules issued by the Seattle Center under the city's authority meet the requirements for valid restrictions on speech under the First Amendment?

DECISION Yes. The U.S. Court of Appeals for the Ninth Circuit reversed the decision of the lower court and remanded the case for further proceedings. "Such content neutral and narrowly tailored rules * * * must be upheld."

REASON The court concluded first that the rules requiring permits and badges were "content neutral." Time, place, and manner restrictions do not violate the First Amendment if they burden all expression equally and do not allow officials to treat different messages differently. In this case, the rules met this test and thus did not discriminate based on content. The court also concluded that the rules were "narrowly tailored" to "promote a substantial government interest that would be achieved less effectively" otherwise. With the rules, the city was trying to "reduce territorial disputes among performers, deter patron harassment, and facilitate the identification and apprehension of offending performers." This was pursuant to the valid governmental objective of protecting the safety and convenience of the other performers and the public generally. The public's complaints about Berger and others showed that unregulated street performances posed a threat to these interests. The court was "satisfied that the city's permit scheme was designed to further valid governmental objectives."

Review of Sample Court Case

Here, we provide a review of the briefed version to indicate the kind of information that is contained in each section.

CITATION The name of the case is *Berger v. City of Seattle*. Berger is the plaintiff; the City of Seattle is the defendant. The U.S. Court of Appeals for the Ninth Circuit decided this case in 2008. The citation states that this case can be found in volume 512 of the Federal Reporter, Third Series, on page 582.

FACTS The *Facts* section identifies the plaintiff and the defendant, describes the events leading up to this suit, the allegations made by the plaintiff in the initial suit, and (because this case is an appellate court decision) the lower court's ruling and the party appealing. The party appealing's argument on appeal is also sometimes included here.

ISSUE The *Issue* section presents the central issue (or issues) decided by the court. In this case, the U.S. Court of Appeals for the Ninth Circuit considered whether certain rules imposed on street performers by local government authorities satisfied the requirements for valid restrictions on speech under the First Amendment to the U.S. Constitution.

DECISION The *Decision* section includes the court's decision on the issues before it. The decision reflects the opinion of the judge or justice hearing the case. Decisions by appellate courts are frequently phrased in reference to the lower court's decision. In other words, the appellate court may "affirm" the lower court's ruling or "reverse" it. Here, the court determined that Seattle's rules were "content neutral" and "narrowly tailored" to "promote a substantial government interest that would otherwise be achieved less effectively." The court found in favor of the city and reversed the lower court's ruling in the plaintiff's (Berger's) favor.

REASON The *Reason* section includes references to the relevant laws and legal principles that the court applied in coming to its conclusion in the case. The relevant law in the *Berger* case included the requirements under the First Amendment for evaluating the purpose and effect of government regulation with respect to expression. This section also explains the court's application of the law to the facts in this case.

Analyzing Case Problems

In addition to learning how to brief cases, students of business law and the legal environment also find it helpful to know how to analyze case problems. Part of the study of business law and the legal environment usually involves analyzing case problems, such as those included in this text at the end of each chapter.

For each case problem in this book, we provide the relevant background and facts of the lawsuit and the issue before the court. When you are assigned one of these problems, your job will be to determine how the court should decide the issue, and why. In other words, you will need to engage in legal analysis and reasoning. Here, we offer some suggestions on how to make this task less daunting. We begin by presenting a sample problem:

> While Janet Lawson, a famous pianist, was shopping in Quality Market, she slipped and fell on a wet floor in one of the aisles. The floor had recently been mopped by one of the store's employees, but there were no signs warning customers that the floor in that area was wet. As a result of the fall, Lawson injured her right arm and was unable to perform piano concerts for the next six months. Had she been able to perform the scheduled concerts, she would have earned approximately $60,000 over that period of time. Lawson sued Quality Market for this amount, plus another $10,000 in medical expenses. She claimed that the store's failure to warn customers of the wet floor constituted negligence and therefore the market was liable for her injuries. Will the court agree with Lawson? Discuss.

Understand the Facts

This may sound obvious, but before you can analyze or apply the relevant law to a specific set of facts, you must clearly understand those facts. In other words, you should read through the case problem carefully—more than once, if necessary—to make sure you understand the identity of the plaintiff(s) and defendant(s) in the case and the progression of events that led to the lawsuit.

In the sample case problem just given, the identity of the parties is fairly obvious. Janet Lawson is the one bringing the suit; therefore, she is the plaintiff. Quality Market, against whom she is bringing the suit, is the defendant. Some of the case problems you may work on have multiple plaintiffs or defendants. Often, it is helpful to use abbreviations for the parties. To indicate a reference to a plaintiff, for example, the *pi* symbol—π—is often used, and a defendant is denoted by a delta—Δ—a triangle.

The events leading to the lawsuit are also fairly straightforward. Lawson slipped and fell on a wet floor, and she contends that Quality Market should be liable for her injuries because it was negligent in not posting a sign warning customers of the wet floor.

When you are working on case problems, realize that the facts should be accepted as they are given. For example, in our sample problem, it should be accepted that the floor was wet and that there was no sign. In other words, avoid making conjectures, such as "Maybe the floor wasn't too wet," or "Maybe an employee was getting a sign to put up," or "Maybe someone stole the sign." Questioning the facts as they are presented only adds confusion to your analysis.

Legal Analysis and Reasoning

Once you understand the facts given in the case problem, you can begin to analyze the case. Recall from the previous Part that the IRAC method is a helpful tool to use in the legal analysis and reasoning process. IRAC is an acronym for **I**ssue, **R**ule, **A**pplication, **C**onclusion. **A**pplying this method to our sample problem would involve the following steps:

1 First, you need to decide what legal *issue* is involved in the case. In our sample case, the basic issue is whether Quality Market's failure to warn customers of the wet floor constituted negligence. As discussed before, negligence is a *tort*—a civil wrong. In a tort lawsuit, the plaintiff seeks to be compensated for another's wrongful act. A defendant will be deemed negligent if he or she breached a duty of care owed to the plaintiff and the breach of that duty caused the plaintiff to suffer harm.

2 Once you have identified the issue, the next step is to determine what **rule of law** applies to the issue. To make this determination, you will want to review carefully the text of the chapter in which the relevant rule of law for the problem appears. Our sample case problem involves the tort of negligence. The applicable rule of law is the tort law principle that business owners owe a duty to exercise reasonable care to protect their customers (*business invitees*). Reasonable care, in this context, includes either removing—or warning customers of—*foreseeable* risks about which the owner *knew* or *should have known*. Business owners need

not warn customers of "open and obvious" risks, however. If a business owner breaches this duty of care (fails to exercise the appropriate degree of care toward customers), and the breach of duty causes a customer to be injured, the business owner will be liable to the customer for the customer's injuries.

3 The next—and usually the most difficult—step in analyzing case problems is the **application** of the relevant rule of law to the specific facts of the case you are studying. In our sample problem, applying the tort law principle just discussed presents few difficulties. An employee of the store had mopped the floor in the aisle where Lawson slipped and fell, but no sign was present indicating that the floor was wet. That a customer might fall on a wet floor is clearly a foreseeable risk. Therefore, the failure to warn customers about the wet floor was a breach of the duty of care owed by the business owner to the store's customers.

4 Once you have completed Step 3 in the IRAC method, you should be ready to draw your **conclusion**. In our sample problem, Quality Market is liable to Lawson for her injuries, because the market's breach of its duty of care caused Lawson's injuries.

The fact patterns in the case problems presented in this text are not always as simple as those presented in our sample problem. Often, for example, a case has more than one plaintiff or defendant. A case may also involve more than one issue and have more than one applicable rule of law. Furthermore, in some case problems the facts may indicate that the general rule of law should not apply. For example, suppose that a store employee advised Lawson not to walk on the floor in the aisle because it was wet, but Lawson decided to walk on it anyway. This fact could alter the outcome of the case because the store could then raise the defense of *assumption of risk*. Nonetheless, a careful review of the chapter should always provide you with the knowledge you need to analyze the problem thoroughly and arrive at accurate conclusions.

APPENDIX B
HOW TO READ A U.S. SUPREME COURT OPINION

Reading a U.S. Supreme Court opinion can be intimidating. The average opinion includes 4,751 words, and is one of approximately 75 issued each year. It might be reassuring, however, to know that opinions contain similar parts and tend to follow a similar format. There are also useful things to identify amid the pages to help focus reading. Here is a basic guide for reading a U.S. Supreme Court opinion.

1. Identify the Parts

Typically, a U.S. Supreme Court opinion is comprised of one or more, or all, of the following parts:

- **Syllabus**

The syllabus appears first, before the main opinion. It is not part of the official opinion, but rather, a summary added by the Court to help the reader better understand the case and the decision. The syllabus outlines the facts of the case and the path that the case has taken to get to the Supreme Court. The last portion of the syllabus sometimes summarizes which justice authored the main opinion, which justices joined in the main opinion, and which justices might have issued concurring or dissenting opinions.

- **Main Opinion**

Following the syllabus is the main opinion. This is the Court's *official* decision in the case. In legal terms, the opinion announces a decision and provides an explanation for the decision by articulating the legal rationale that the justices relied upon to reach the decision. The main opinion may take different forms, depending on how the justices decide certain issues.

Sometimes decisions are unanimous—all of the justices agree and offer one rationale for their decision, so the Court issues one *unanimous opinion*. When more than half of the justices agree, the Court issues a *majority opinion*. Other times, there is no majority, but a plurality, so the Court issues a *plurality opinion*. Typically, one justice is identified as the author of the main opinion. *Per curiam* opinions, however, do not identify any authors, and are simply, opinions of the Court.

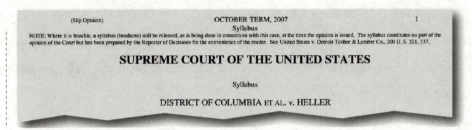

• **Concurring and Dissenting Opinions**

Often, there are multiple opinions within the document because the justices are not in agreement. Justices who agree with the result of the main opinion, or the resolution of the dispute between the two parties, but base their decision on a different rationale may issue one or more *concurring opinion(s)*. Likewise, justices who disagree with the main opinion in both result and legal rationale may issue one or more *dissenting opinion(s)*.

2. Understand the Formal Elements

Regardless of which, or how many, parts comprise the opinion, they will share several formal elements. Headings typically include the Court term in which the opinion was announced, case docket number, argument dates, and decision date. Another important element is the case name, which helps determine the parties involved in the case (see sidebar). Finally, there might be an explanation of where the case came from before reaching the Court. Often, there is a note about certiorari, an order by which a higher court reviews the decision of a lower court. For example, an opinion may reference "Certiorari for the United States Court of Appeals for the Ninth Circuit." That means the Court reviewed the case from the lower court, the U.S. Court of Appeals

of the Ninth Circuit.

3. Read Purposefully

When reading an opinion, it is important to focus on a few "big picture" takeaways:

• **Facts**

Pinpoint the facts of the case, or the "story" —who, what, when, and where. Supreme Court cases tend to begin with a person, place, thing, or event, often in everyday scenarios. The goal is to be able to tell the story of the case, including its procedural history.

• **Legal Dispute(s)**

What are the legal issues in the case? What questions are being presented? Is the Court interpreting the Constitution or a statute—e.g. an act of Congress? Try to identify the parties' particular dispute(s) and their main arguments.

• **Disposition**

Generally, the end of the main opinion includes the disposition, or what action the Court is taking. When reviewing decisions from a lower court, the Supreme Court basically has three options:

• **Affirm** — allow the lower court's ruling to stand;

• **Reverse, Void, or Vacate** — overturn the lower court's ruling; or

• **Remand** — send the case back to a lower court for a retrial.

Sometimes the Court combines the last two of these options—reverse and remand—and not only overturns the lower court's decision, but also orders a retrial.

• **Law**

The main opinion will include a section on law, which includes the Court's legal reasoning or holding. In some opinions, this will be clearer than others, but try to identify at least one principle of law that the Court outlines as a basis for its ruling. Sometimes, the opinion cites past cases—legal precedent, policy, or outlines other considerations. Finally, were there any concurring or dissenting opinions? If so, try to determine the differences in reasoning.

- **Significance and Scope**

Consider the significance of the opinion. This may not be readily apparent simply from reading the text of the opinion. What do you think will be its application beyond the particular facts of the case? Consider other possible fact patterns to which it might apply. What else do you think will be the consequence of the opinion, especially considering its holding or legal reasoning? What precedent might it establish?

For more information about reading U.S. Supreme Court opinions, including a document map and explanations of key terms, please visit www.insightsmagazine.org.

What Does That Case Citation Mean?

Each of the pieces of the case citation mean something, as illustrated below:

Gideon v. Wainwright 372 U.S. 375 (1963)
     1   2   3   4   5

1 Case name

2 Volume of the report series in which the full decision is officially documented

3 Name of the report series in which the decision is documented: "U.S." stands for the *U.S. Report*, which is printed by the Supreme Court. Sometimes a case name refers to an independently published series, such as "S. Ct.," which refers to the *Supreme Court Reporter* published by West Publishing.

4 Page number in the referenced volume on which the decision begins

5 Year the opinion was released

A Note on Case Names

Cases are named according to the parties involved. When there are two parties, the first name is the petitioner, or the party filing the lawsuit against the second party, the respondent.

Sometimes case names do not list two parties, such as cases whose names include *In re* or *Ex parte*. *In re* is a Latin term meaning "in the matter of" and is typically used in cases where there are not two designated adversarial parties. Such cases might involve property disputes, court orders, or situations where the Court is asked to clarify matters, such as *In re Debs*. In this example, Debs was challenging an injunction, or court order, issued by the federal government during a labor strike. The term is also used in certain cases involving juveniles, such as *In re Gault*.

Ex parte is also a Latin term, which refers to a case "from one party." Typically, one or more of the parties is absent from the legal proceedings. *Ex parte* is followed by the name of the party who initiated the case, as in *Ex parte Merryman*. One individual, Merryman, arrested during the Civil War, challenged the government's right to hold him without charges. He sought an order that would require the government to charge him with something, or let him go.

Locating Supreme Court Opinions

• **U.S. Supreme Court**

www.supremecourt.gov/opinions

The Court posts opinions for the current term as well as PDF copies of bound volumes of opinions from previous terms.

• **Legal Information Institute**

www.law.cornell.edu

Comprehensive site from Cornell University Law School that offers opinions and notes "significant" cases from each term.

• **Oyez Project**

www.oyez.org

Managed by the Illinois Institute of Technology Chicago-Kent College of Law and offers opinions, audio of oral argument, and summary analysis of each opinion.

APPENDIX C
TRANSCRIPT OF A RECORDING OF A TELEPHONE CONVERSATION BETWEEN THE PRESIDENT AND H.R. HALDEMAN, THE WHITE HOUSE TELEPHONE, APRIL 19, 1973, FROM 9:37 P.M. TO 9:53 P.M.

PRESIDENT: Haldeman please.

OPERATOR: (Unintelligible) Thank you.(Pause)

PRESIDENT: Hello

HALDEMAN: Yes sir.

PRESIDENT: Bob?

HALDEMAN: Yes sir.

PRESIDENT: Oh hi. I talked to the two boys here.

HALDEMAN: Couple of characters, aren't, they?

PRESIDENT: They really are, but I was very useful, very interesting. I say ah, they didn't, they only had a half hour with the uh, U.S. Attorneys...

HALDEMAN: Yeah.

PRESIDENT: ...and they say stand firm.

HALDEMAN: Ha ha. They had a sh...

PRESIDENT: Yeah.

HALDEMAN: ...short session. Apparently they had—those guys had a busy day. They had Hunt in there and all this (unintelligible) breaking on the...

PRESIDENT: Yeah. What is up? Have you ever found out what the hell it is?

HALDEMAN: No. Just that, I haven't found out and I don't know if anyone knows or not. Nobody seems to have any idea what it is.

Ehrlichman had some (unintelligible) on it that it was, that, was offered to Silbert at some point and he didn't want it. Whish has put him in a very awkward

HALDEMAN CONT.: position which is lie is on.. He's denouncing all thetiqhole story as preposterous.

PRESIDENT: (Unintelligible) denouncing it.

HALDEMAN: Silbert is, yeah.

PRESIDENT: (Unintelligible) What is this? Eight cases of stuff that was carried out of the White House. Is that what it is?

HALDEMAN: That's what they say. Out of Hunt's, it was the contents of Hunt's desk.

PRESIDENT: Eight cases?

HALDEMAN: Ha ha. Six cases I guess.

PRESIDENT: Oh, that's what it is.

HALDEMAN: Six cartons (unintelligible)

PRESIDENT: And carried to where, to an apartment?

HALDEMAN: It was taken to someplace where it was stored somewhere by this guy's client. This guy's a lawyer who's telling the story. He says his client stored it for the summer and then returned it to the Committee to Re-elect just before the election.

PRESIDENT: (Unintelligible) that have been, hmm?

HALDEMAN: Which is weird story.

PRESIDENT: They have it now then. They have the material?

HALDEMAN: (Unintelligible) they don't. I don't know where the material is. (Unintelligible) apparently as, as all this stuff is coming out this guy's scared he's going to get hung on an obstruction of justice thing and so he's going in and filing notice that, that ah he knew about this…

PRESIDENT: Who is the guy, Bob? Is he somebody that worked for the Committee

APPENDIX C
TRANSCRIPT OF A RECORDING OF A TELEPHONE CONVERSATION BETWEEN THE PRESIDENT AND H.R. HALDEMAN, THE WHITE HOUSE TELEPHONE, APRIL 19, 1973, FROM 9:37 P.M. TO 9:53 P.M.

or...

HALDEMAN: It's a lawyer. I don't know who his client is.

PRESIDENT: That's w hat I meant. Who's the client?

HALDEMAN: I don't know. I haven't any idea who his client is. He ah, he won't say. (Pause) That's very strange.

PRESIDENT: Colson doesn't really know?

HALDEMAN: I don't know. I haven't, ah, John Ehrlichman talked to Colson about it so he may have more of a reading on it.

PRESIDENT: (Unintelligible) just another — another one of those things.

HALDEMAN: (Unintelligible) run all the way through with John. We have another one that, that ah, the <u>Post</u> going to tell the story tomorrow.

PRESIDENT: Yeah.

HALDEMAN: This is an associate of John Deans', who is seeking to make John Dean's version of this whole thing public so that Dean, in his testimony before the Grand Jury will implicate people above and below himself and will state that Haldeman engineered a cover-up to hide the involvement of a pre presidential aides in the (unintelligible) operation, and that one close associate said that Dean is prepared to tell whatever that ah, whatever role he might have played in the Watergate case came as a result of orders from superiors in the White House, despite the allegations Dean had no advance knowledge of the bugging, that the truth is long and broad and it goes up and down, higher and lower, and that they can't make a case that this was just Mitchell and Dean. Dean will welcome the opportunity to tell his side to the Grand Jury. He's not going to go down in flames for the activities of others. The <u>Post</u> called the White House for comment on that...

PRESIDENT: Oh boy.

HALDEMAN: ...tried to reach me, I guess, for comment. (unintelligible).

PRESIDENT: Yeah.

HALDEMAN: And ah (unintelligible) this guy, that he called, he tried to reach Dean and finally got through to him and he's having his calls screened by Fielding and he's hiding in a hotel somewhere. Dean called him back…

PRESIDENT: Yeah.

HALDEMAN: And ah, Ron gave him the story and Dean said his first comment was "Oh fuck." And then he said I sus…I have a pretty good suspicion who it is and he's got things scrambled. I never mentioned Haldeman. I just said higher up and (unintelligible) apparently. And he said, then Ron said will "Why don't you call the Post and (unintelligible)…

PRESIDENT: Yeah.

HALDEMAN: …the story's not true before they run it. Dean said "Well Ron there's some fact and some fiction in it and (unintelligible) call them and deny it." And ah, he said why, Dean then said to Ron "Why don't you call the Post and say that they can't run the story unless Dean confirms it and Dean hasn't confirmed it." Ron said "That's ridiculous John and you know it. They won't (unintelligible) suggested that Dean have Fielding call the Post and handle it. And Dean said "Well I, maybe I can do that. I want you to know I'm not playing games. This is a fishing type story and they're just trying to smoke something out." A w-, later Dean called Ron back, just a minute ago as a matter of fact, and he said " I can't call the Post, but why don't you Ron? Call the guy from the Post and say that you have talked with me and that at no time did I say that Haldeman was in" (unintelligible) (Pause)

PRESIDENT: Well, so (unintelligible)

HALDEMAN: So Ron's going to try that but…

PRESIDENT: Yeah.

HALDEMAN: …he's afraid that Dean cleverly waited 'til 9:30 to tell him that so that it

APPENDIX C

TRANSCRIPT OF A RECORDING OF A TELEPHONE CONVERSATION BETWEEN THE PRESIDENT AND H.R. HALDEMAN, THE WHITE HOUSE TELEPHONE, APRIL 19, 1973, FROM 9:37 P.M. TO 9:53 P.M.

would be too late to change the story.

PRESIDENT: (Unintelligible) this is a—Look Bob, these are the things we, we, we sort of expect this don't we?

HALDEMAN: Sure.

PRESIDENT: …the Dean thing. And ah, we just stand firm on it. That's all, don't you agree? What the hell else can you do?

HALDEMAN: I don't think, I don't think we want to (unintelligible), more of it lying down than we have to.

PRESIDENT: I agree, I agree, I—except I don't know what the hell to do with Dean, that's the problem, isn't that it?

HALDEMAN: Dean's obviously got other people playing his game now, that are tougher than he intends to.

PRESIDENT: His lawyer probably, huh?

HALDEMAN: I would say his lawyer, yeah.

PRESIDENT: His associates up and down, huh. Was he referring to Ehrlichman and you and who the, whose down?

HALDEMAN: Well, Colson…

PRESIDENT: Colson, of course.

HALDEMAN: Or it could be people over at the Committee or ah, you know, LaRue and Mitchell…

PRESIDENT: Mitchell, right.

HALDEMAN: All sorts of people.

PRESIDENT: Your fellows, I asked them their judgment and they said that (unintelligible) for whatever it's worth, I mean they don't buy the Garment theory. Da, you know.

HALDEMAN: You mean - on, on our taking any action now.

PRESIDENT: One might, ah, yes, on…

HALDEMAN: On you taking any action now.

PRESIDENT: …on resigning. They said, well, just have to, course with all this, you have to remember they said that they didn't see that it would, they, they, they, they just, ah, it would be uh, admission of guilt, that's what they'ed say.

HALDEMAN: Well, I think they're right.

PRESIDENT: That's the point, so ah, we're going to have to fight it out.

HALDEMAN: An admission of guilt (unintelligible) as long as everywhere else really, really screws things up.

PRESIDENT: But the point is that what you do is to let them run their story and then ah, ah, their stories and so forth and so on, but then we have to play it as they say, day by day and the U.S. Attorney is uh, is confronted with a tough choice, whether he's gonna indict or put you on a list of non-indictable people.

HALDEMAN: Or nothing at all, which is what they think he's going to do.

PRESIDENT: At this moment, yes.

HALDEMAN: Yeah.

PRESIDENT: They don't think he's got corroboration but if he doesn't, why that's, that's fine, and ah…

HALDEMAN: They probably told you they find this whole procedure highly…

PRESIDENT: Yes.

HALDEMAN: …irregular.

PRESIDENT: Yeah, they do, they do, but they say it's done, it's done, it's irregular but it's done.

HALDEMAN: Yeah.

PRESIDENT: Ah…

HALDEMAN: That guy's really an interesting guy.

PRESIDENT: Yeah, he sure is. I like 'em both.

HALDEMAN: I do, too.

APPENDIX C
TRANSCRIPT OF A RECORDING OF A TELEPHONE CONVERSATION BETWEEN THE PRESIDENT AND H.R. HALDEMAN, THE WHITE HOUSE TELEPHONE, APRIL 19, 1973, FROM 9:37 P.M. TO 9:53 P.M.

PRESIDENT: But they ah, but they both say they have, I don't think they've seen these stories, but I mean they aren't going to be effected by stories that come out. I told 'em I said "You're gonna have a hell of a lot of stories here, it's gonna be blasting off." And, ah, I think you gotta expect more of it, don't you?

HALDEMAN: Yeah.

PRESIDENT: Yeah. We just batten down the hatches and take it, isn't that right?

HALDEMAN: I'm not sure how, (Unintelligible)' We've gotta, well, we've gotta get the legal part perfected...

PRESIDENT: Yeah.

HALDEMAN: ...and then we've gotta move on the public...

PRESIDENT: On the PR.

HALDEMAN: ...We can't just hunker down and take it for, for...

PRESIDENT: I.agree, I agree. They, they of course ruled, I didn't talk to 'em about, what, what do they think about your making a statement or something or that sort of thing, they...

HALDEMAN: They're worried about it, but they, see, in their, they're not close to it...

PRESIDENT: Yeah.

HALDEMAN: ...at this point...

PRESIDENT: That's right.

HALDEMAN: ...I think there's, you know, we can...

PRESIDENT: Right.

HALDEMAN: ...probably convince em that that's not a bad idea...

PRESIDENT: Right.

HALDEMAN: ...They've gone over my statement. I've given it to em...

PRESIDENT: Yeah, right, right.

HALDEMAN: ...there have a lot of, they don't have much trouble with it, except in a couple areas...

PRESIDENT: Right, right.

HALDEMAN: …and, ah…

PRESIDENT: Incidentally, are you and John going to Florida?

HALDEMAN: I don't know. We, we were planning to…

PRESIDENT: Yeah.

HALDEMAN: …ah, but the thing with them, we're trying to figure now whether we should or not. It may be that we ought not to be gone this weekend.

PRESIDENT: Ought to work with your attorney.

HALDEMAN: Yeah, yeah.

PRESIDENT: Probably so, probably so, but do what you want. You know, you're certainly welcome.

HALDEMAN: Yeah, well, that, that's very nice.

PRESIDENT: Nice, hell, it's just whatever you want, you know, your…

HALDEMAN: It ah, we were concerned about appearance if we don't go, or if I don't, but I don't really think that matters much, especially…

PRESIDENT: No.

HALDEMAN: …because it's Easter…

PRESIDENT: It's Easter, you're going to stay with your family.

HALDEMAN: No, I hadn't thought about it. And we can just say you're going down to spend Easter with your family and we're spending Easter with our families.

PRESIDENT: That's right. It's a family deal, sure.

HALDEMAN: If we don't go, ah, wha, what we might do if it's okay, is go up to Camp David…

PRESIDENT: Right, right.

HALDEMAN: …for a day or two.

PRESIDENT: Very excellent idea.

HALDEMAN: We've got reporters camping on the door here now…

APPENDIX C

TRANSCRIPT OF A RECORDING OF A TELEPHONE CONVERSATION BETWEEN THE PRESIDENT AND H.R. HALDEMAN, THE WHITE HOUSE TELEPHONE, APRIL 19, 1973, FROM 9:37 P.M. TO 9:53 P.M.

PRESIDENT: Oh Christ, yes, go up to Camp David, Bob.

HALDEMAN: Well, we'll see, but ah...

PRESIDENT: Ah, incidentally, and I, the ah, the Cabinet tomorrow, be sure to be there.

HALDEMAN: Yes sir, don't worry.

PRESIDENT: Don't worry. We're gonna be right there and a lot of (unintelligible) I'll just uh state it out — state out front, you know my own conviction. Don't you think I should to the Cabinet?

HALDEMAN: Yeah, but don't, give your own conviction about you're gonna follow this through, but don't

HALDEMAN CONT: support anybody. Don't say you'll stand by us or anything.

PRESIDENT: Well., why not? I mean that ah...

HALDEMAN: I just don't think you should. Look there are so many weird bounces in this, if one of us gets a bad bounce at some point and has to do something then don't you (unintelligible) in your face.

PRESIDENT: Right. (Unintelligible) I say then, that we've ah, (unintelligible) investigating this whole thing, that I ah...

HALDEMAN: And that I'm not going to mention any names.

PRESIDENT: Any names.

HALDEMAN: Because, because, as I said publicly I will say privately to you. I. I, there is going to be no cover up in this...

PRESIDENT: Right.

HALDEMAN: And ah...

PRESIDENT: And that there's, there never...

HALDEMAN: This is gonna, that uh our record on this investigation is gonna prove that we've done everything we could in the proper fashion.

PRESIDENT: Right. That's what you say.

HALDEMAN: Effecting both the need to prosecute and the need to protect.

PRESIDENT: Right. You'd prefer it and rather, and rather than, rather than to say that I stand by Ehrlichman and Haldeman and that sort of thing, that's what I would (unintelligible)

HALDEMAN: Because, see, the thing is nobody yet has, has(unintelligible) a word about, really about Ehrlichman and and they're now all saying that there is no evidence on me.

PRESIDENT: Until this story that's uh a, Dean, though.

HALDEMAN: Well yeah, that's right, and that's Dean and that, it may not go out.

PRESIDENT: Ah, ah, the Post would use it, don't you think?

HALDEMAN: I don't know, they may not. Tell me what, there's a…

PRESIDENT: It's a dangerous thing.

HALDEMAN: …(unintelligible) being played here. There's a lot of rough games being played here and…it's

PRESIDENT: They may be afraid of the libel?

HALDEMAN: We come out better playing a strong game then we do a weak game, all the way along, but I don't think in that…

PRESIDENT: Yeah.

HALDEMAN: …that you as President should now endorse anybody.

PRESIDENT: (Unintelligible) I guess you're right.

HALDEMAN: Because, in the first place, if you say I…

PRESIDENT: First of all, first…

HALDEMAN: (Unintelligible) Haldeman and (unintelligible) Ehrlichman…

PRESIDENT: What do I say about Mitchell?

HALDEMAN: Then you lea…Well, what do you say about Mitchell, what do you say about Dean?

PRESIDENT: That's right.

HALDEMAN: There's a lot more suspicion on Dean now, are you gonna say you stand by me, but not by…

APPENDIX C
TRANSCRIPT OF A RECORDING OF A TELEPHONE CONVERSATION BETWEEN THE PRESIDENT AND H.R. HALDEMAN, THE WHITE HOUSE TELEPHONE, APRIL 19, 1973, FROM 9:37 P.M. TO 9:53 P.M.

PRESIDENT: That's right, that's right. And if Is if I say that, then Dean says, "What the hell, why don't I stand by him?"

HALDEMAN: You could say, "I'm not gonna mention any names, but I would caution any of you to come to any conclusions about any individuals..."

PRESIDENT: Yeah, that's right.

HALDEMAN: ...because there are a lot of those charges in here as well as some valid ones...

PRESIDENT: That's right, that's right.

HALDEMAN: ...and until they are properly sorted out, it would be very wise for everybody to keep his mouth shut...

PRESIDENT: Right.

HALDEMAN: ...and, and his open mind.

PRESIDENT: Right, right, right, right, right, right. That's good, Bob, that's good. Well, that's ah, this thing about this stuff and Hunt stuff that was carted up, I don't know what now...

HALDEMAN: (Unintelligible) It's incredible. This ah, this thing is so frigging bizarre that it's, it's beyond...

PRESIDENT: Yeah, but, but, but, you say Silbert, what does he say about it, I, I didn't hear that...

HALDEMAN: Well Ehrlichman has some story, I guess he got from Colson, saying that it was this material was offered to Silbert at some point. They said they'd give it to him and he said he didn't want it, and that puts him in a very sticky wicket now that it's known that it exists, so he has said this story that this lawyer had it, ah that this lawyer's client had it for, for all through the summer, it's preposterous. It's kind of a stupid thing for him to say. There's

HALDEMAN CONT: no point in his saying anything. He over-reacted, I guess, to this, and ah, lawyers may have told you when they talked with Silbert today, they said he was very up-tight…

PRESIDENT: mmmm.

HALDEMAN: …and ah; very formal and…

PRESIDENT: Yeah.

HALDEMAN: …and obviously (unintelligible) harassed. (Unintelligible) know Silbert very well though, they know…

PRESIDENT: But, but.Silbert, yeah, they've only met him once. Does (Unintelligible) the, the, the law, ah, the lawyer says that he offered it to Silbert, is that the story?

HALDEMAN: No, (unintelligible) Colson says, so Colson obviously must know something about this and I think John, I, I didn't get the full fill on this 'cause John came in at the end of the meeting (unintelligible) and (unintelligible) in and, ah…

PRESIDENT: Uh huh, Colson ah, se- that it was offered to Silbert and…

HALDEMAN: Yeah.

PRESIDENT: It was contents of his safe?

HALDEMAN: (Unintelligible)

PRESIDENT: His office.

HALDEMAN: (Unintelligible) his office (unintelligible) safe obviously cause his safe they didn't get in so, and it doesn't, they didn't, they said that things from his desk…

PRESIDENT: Yeah.

HALDEMAN: From Hunt's desk. It was the next morning. See,

HALDEMAN CONT: that could be Colson, who was worried about the safe as I recall…

PRESIDENT: Yeah.

HALDEMAN: …too, who may have told somebody, you know, "For heaven sake get

APPENDIX C
TRANSCRIPT OF A RECORDING OF A TELEPHONE CONVERSATION BETWEEN THE PRESIDENT AND H.R. HALDEMAN, THE WHITE HOUSE TELEPHONE, APRIL 19, 1973, FROM 9:37 P.M. TO 9:53 P.M.

over there and, and ah, do something."

PRESIDENT: Yeah.

HALDEMAN: Well…

PRESIDENT: Anyway…

HALDEMAN: We gotta be careful not to draw conclusions.

PRESIDENT: That's right.

HALDEMAN: You just really don't know.

PRESIDENT: We don't know, that's right.

HALDEMAN: And it would be awful unfair to somebody by…

PRESIDENT: That's right, I couldn't agree more.

HALDEMAN: By skipping something.

PRESIDENT: That's what, we're not going to do that. Well, it's ah, it's certainly, the difficult one here to figure out is Dean, isn't it?

HALDEMAN: Yes, sir.

PRESIDENT: God damn him, he's ah, I don't know what ah, what…

HALDEMAN: He's totally distorted in his own mind now and he, he…

PRESIDENT: Yeah.

HALDEMAN: …consequently I guess, very dangerous…

PRESIDENT: Yeah.

HALDEMAN: …But ah, sort of pathetic at the same time.

PRESIDENT: Yeah, yeah trying to save himself.

HALDEMAN: (Unintelligible) moorings and his, ah, you know…

PRESIDENT: (Unintelligible) saying anything.

HALDEMAN: …swinging out in all kinds of ways.

PRESIDENT: That's right. Okay.

HALDEMAN: We'll just have to see.

PRESIDENT: That's right, thank you.

HALDEMAN: Okay.